PRESENTATIONS

Second Edition

PRESENTATIONS

Second Edition

Proven Techniques for Creating Presentations That Get Results

Gary McClain, Ph.D.

BUSINESS

AVON, MASSACHUSETTS

Published by Adams Media, an F+W Publications Company
57 Littlefield Street
Avon, MA 02322
www.adamsmedia.com

Produced by Amaranth Illuminare.

ISBN-10: 1-59869-153-8
ISBN-13: 9-781-59869-153-5

Printed in Canada.

J I H G F E D C B A

Library of Congress Cataloging-in-Publication Data
McClain, Gary R.
Presentations / Gary McClain. — 2nd ed.
p.   cm.
Includes bibliographical references and index.
ISBN-13: 978-1-59869-153-5 (pbk.)
ISBN-10: 1-59869-153-8 (pbk.)
1. Business presentations. I. Title.
HF5718.22.M33 2007
658.4'52—dc22   2007010856

This book is available at quantity discounts for bulk purchases.
For information, please call 1-800-289-0963.

Contents

Introduction ix

1. Your Purpose 1
   The First Triangle: Your Foundation 2
   Your Presentation's Purpose 3
   Why You? 3
   Why This Presentation? 7
   Objectives and Expectations 7
   Types of Presentations 8
   Informational 9
   Motivational 15
   Persuasive 17
   Sales 18

2. Your Audience 21
   The View from Center Stage 22
   Your Peers 23
   Your Superiors 27
   Subordinates 30
   Willing Participants 32
   Mandatory Attendance 33
   Remote 35
   Special Needs 36
   Stakeholders and Hidden Audiences 37

3. **Your Topic**.. 41
    Audience Knowledge about Your Topic 43
    Your Knowledge about Your Topic 44
    Research 46
    Details and Facts 49
    Buzzwords and Jargon............................. 51
    Anecdotes and Stories............................ 52
    Copyright Matters 54

4. **Developing Your Presentation**..................... 57
    What's Your Style? A Quiz 57
    Your Comfort Zone................................ 62
    Logical Progression 63
    Time and Environment............................ 66
    Media Options 67
    Handouts... 70
    Visuals... 72
    Your Notes....................................... 72
    Anticipating Questions and Challenges 74

5. **Preparing Yourself**............................... 77
    You're the Expert!................................ 77
    Attire 79
    Demeanor 83
    Be Yourself 85
    Practice, Practice, Practice 87
    The Myth of Winging It........................... 90

6. **Rehearsal**....................................... 93
    First Run: Read-Through 94
    Second Run: How Do You Sound? 97
    Third Run: How Do You Look?..................... 103
    Gaps and Glitches 107

7. **Pre-Presentation Checklist**.........................**109**
    Lists and Post-Its 109
    Production Schedule 112
    Tasks and People 118
    Confirmations 119
    Logistics.. 121
    Supplies 126
    Your Presenter's Tool Bag 127
    Contingency Planning.............................. 128

8. **Show Time!** **131**
    Setting Up 131
    And Now, Our Main Feature 134
    Greeting Your Audience 134
    Establishing Expectations........................... 136
    Introducing Your Presentation....................... 138
    Delivering Your Presentation........................ 140
    Audience Participation 143
    Fielding Questions................................. 145
    Concluding Your Presentation....................... 148

9. **Handling Challenges**...........................**151**
    Keep Your Sense of Humor 151
    Late Arrivals and Early Departures................... 153
    Interruptions...................................... 155
    Inattentive Audience 157
    Argumentative Participants 159
    Defusing Hostility and Anger 161
    Saboteurs... 163
    Show Stealers 164

10. **Evaluating Your Success** **167**
    The Value of Feedback.............................. 168
    Informal Assessment............................... 171
    Structured Assessment 173

Sample Evaluation Forms 175
Sample Evaluation Form #1:
   Numeric Scale with Comments 175
Sample Evaluation Form #2:
   Narrative Responses 177
Follow Up with Participants 177
Follow Up with Stakeholders 178
When Things Truly Did Go Badly 180
Incorporating Improvements 182
On to the Next Presentation! 184

Appendix A: Resources **187**

Appendix B: Further Reading **189**

Appendix C: Quotations for Speeches **191**

Index **207**

Introduction

What was the best presentation you ever sat through? What was great about it? How did it affect you? I've sat through some great ones over the years, from scientists, politicians, journalists. And while they differed greatly from each other, they all had one thing in common. I left my world, at least for a few minutes, and entered into theirs. Were they all naturally gifted? Probably not. But they had mastered the art of presenting, most likely learned over time.

I often do presentations on the basis of my credentials. When I first started doing that, I had a PowerPoint slide that said something along the lines of, "I have made every possible mistake." That slide was so subject to interpretation—often in ways I didn't expect or intend—that I yanked it out. But what I wanted to get across was that the best way to learn is by sticking your neck out and taking chances, and learning from your mistakes. While this would not be the best way to do brain surgery, or any number of other professions, it is one of the ways that people often learn to do presentations.

Presentations are a blend of science and art. There is a science, a conventional wisdom, that governs how presentations are given. You will read a lot of this science in this book: how to organize your material, how to make sure you've thought of all the details at your presentation venue, how to handle questions. By carefully following the guidelines, you'll have all of this handled. And as a new presenter, when you have all of the science taken care of, you'll have a lot more time and energy to work on the art. Which is really the fun stuff, in my opinion.

The art side of presentations is that magic that comes about from a mixture of understanding what your audience needs to hear and the best way for them to hear it. It's making the emotional connection, establishing the rapport, that makes your audience want to listen to you. You're so compelling, you make every person out there feel like you are giving everything you can because they are so important. The art takes more practice, not only in terms of practicing the immediate presentation, but also applying your own experiences to the presentations that follow.

You perfect the science of presentations by focusing on the details and making sure each one is covered. But you perfect the art of presentations by forgetting about yourself, avoiding self-consciousness, and focusing on what the audience needs. This is learned over time, one presentation after another, a journey of experience and discovery. Then one day you'll step in front of your audience and suddenly realize you've arrived. But don't get too comfortable. Even the most seasoned presenters tell me that they consider themselves a work in progress. We're always learning to be better. This book is intended to get you started on your own path.

The prospect of doing a presentation can be overwhelming when you look at the whole of it. So I've structured this book around a pattern of triangles. Architecturally, the triangle is both simple and strong. When all three legs are firmly grounded, the triangle provides fairly rock solid support—it takes a lot to knock it over. The same is true of presentations.

The first three chapters cover the foundation elements of your presentation—purpose, audience, and topic; the first triangle. The next three chapters cover the process of developing your presentation, from research through rehearsal—the second triangle. Chapter 7 is an interlude of sorts, your "Pre-Presentation Checklist." The final three chapters—and final triangle—cover the three phases of the presentation itself.

I hope this book will let you learn from some of my mistakes so you won't have to make them yourself. So I share both my mistakes and my solutions for remedying them. I also give you my version of the conventional wisdom that guides all presenters. You'll make a few of your own gaffes, certainly, as you develop your own style as a presenter. That's part of the learning process, after all.

Anyone can be a good presenter. All you have to do is follow the guidelines for what makes a good presentation, learn how to infuse your presentation with your personality, and practice. People often tell me that they don't think they can do good presentations. They don't know whether the audience will find them interesting. They aren't good joke tellers. They can't stay awake during someone else's presentation, so why should they believe other people will stay awake during theirs?

When people give me those excuses, I ask them where they got these ideas. Usually, they give me an example of the last really great or really bad presentation they sat through. It's as if it's then somehow ordained that they must present exactly like that great presenter, or that their presentation is inevitably going to be as bad as the one they hated. You don't have to be like the great presenter—in fact, you really shouldn't try because it won't be *you*. You don't have to make the same mistakes as the dreadful presenter, either—that's not you. But you can learn from both.

There is no better way to really put yourself out there—among your coworkers, management, clients, outside groups—than to create and deliver a presentation. You are doing much more than just imparting some knowledge, updating on the news, teaching a skill. You are displaying your enthusiasm, knowledge, personal style, insights. This is really an opportunity to present who you are and what you are about.

Let's face it—while scary and risky and all of that, presenting is also affirming and gratifying. And with some hard work and practice, and willingness to accept and integrate criticism, you can become an excellent presenter. And everyone in the audience knows that doing the presentation is giving you this opportunity. They may not show it, but they envy you this opportunity.

Presenting also provides you with the opportunity to create a meaningful connection with a group of people—rapport. As the presenter, you establish a relationship that provides a basis for you to present your material and for the audience to accept this message. Your presentation then has the potential to influence the audience well beyond your immediate words—even to change their perceptions of you.

By being a presenter, you are entering a whole new realm of professionalism. You are moving from the back office to the front office. Be patient with yourself. Have fun. You wouldn't be here if you weren't ready for it.

Chapter 1

Your Purpose

I love to develop and give presentations. I even seek out opportunities to give presentations. A presentation is a way for me to connect with my audience—people who might be clients or potential clients, people who have a need and that only I can, at least when I am giving the presentation, be the person who can meet that need. I enjoy this connection. My audience benefits from the presentation, and so do I.

But it hasn't always been this way. For many years I fumbled and stumbled my way through presentations, dreading—and sometimes even trying to dodge—assignments that required them. Presentations were very time-consuming and for the most part seemed pointless. I didn't see any greater purpose beyond the torture and torment of me and my audience, and often I couldn't see which of us was getting the worse end of it.

I never knew where to start, so when preparing my presentation often I started in the middle and worked until I boxed myself into a corner. I put in hours and hours, most of them wasted. Because my presentations were not well organized or well rehearsed, during the presentation I often would suddenly find myself repeating something that I knew I had already said. Or in the middle of a concept that I had never really thought through when I was developing the presentation, and then trying to stammer my way out of it. When I stood in front of an audience, I felt like I was standing in front of a judge and jury—people who didn't want to be there any more than I did, and were waiting for me to make a big enough blunder that they could finally conclude I had nothing to offer. I would walk away not really knowing what my major points were and, worse yet, not sure if the audience did. And as you can conclude, I had some experiences that weren't exactly stellar. All because I didn't have the fundamentals in place.

Fundamentals matter in everything you do—driving a car, playing sports, cooking, writing a book, and of course preparing and delivering presentations. These are the core basics, the foundation upon which everything else builds. Where your foundation goes, your performance follows: Solid foundation, solid performance. Shaky foundation, shaky performance. Sure, you might luck out once in a while and get a great performance from a mediocre foundation. But my guess is, you're reading this book because you know good presentations require more than good luck.

THE FIRST TRIANGLE: YOUR FOUNDATION

In the Introduction, I told you we would build upon a series of triangles—an architectural form of strength and support—to make presentations effective, easy, and even fun for you to do. The first of these triangles is the fundamentals of purpose, audience, and topic—the why, who, and what that frame your presentation. Here, in chapter 1, we explore your purpose—why you are doing a presentation. In chapter 2, we look at your audience—the people who will hear and see your presentation. And in chapter 3, we investigate your topic—what you have to say to your audience. This triangle of key elements—purpose, audience, and topic—provides similar strength and support for your presentation. This triangle anchors you.

YOUR PRESENTATION'S PURPOSE

A presentation's purpose determines the content, format, materials, tone, and sometimes even the audience for the presentation. The two questions that may come first to your mind when you find yourself tapped to give a presentation, though you may ask them in frustration and fear, are actually the two questions that may define your presentation's purpose:

- Why me?
- Why this presentation?

The answers to these questions keep the presentation—and you, its presenter—on track and on target. Sounds simple enough, doesn't it? Most of the time, it is. Sometimes, however, you have to dig a little deeper to find the answers . . . and what you find is that there are more answers than you expected. It's worth the effort to ferret them out. The better you understand your presentation's purpose, the more effectively you can prepare.

WHY YOU?

In the early (some say developmental) stages of my professional life, I often was designated to do presentations. Each time I had to, and I emphasize had to because I certainly did not step forward to volunteer, I used to ask myself, "why me?" Presentations were really time-consuming. Here I was, struggling along under the burden of an already heavy workload, and now I was being pulled out of line to pile on still more. And what was the point, anyway? My audience didn't want to be out there any more than I wanted to be standing in front of them. Enough, already! Of course, I could say this only to myself, and not out loud.

I finally discovered that a big part of the answer to "why me?" was in my hands. I could decide that giving a presentation was an opportunity for me, even if it was being forced on me or I received it by default. You can make the same decision, and suddenly "why me?" becomes a matter of fortuitous serendipity. You, amongst all your coworkers and colleagues, have received an opportunity to better define who you are and how you think, both an image builder and an intellectual challenge. You have an opportunity to promote yourself, within your organization as well as among your customers. And you have an opportunity to develop and exhibit your leadership skills. Of course, there also are tangible and practical reasons that you've been selected to make a presentation.

You Have Expertise

One of the most common reasons people are asked (or delegated) to do presentations is that they have particular expertise or knowledge in the subject. Your purpose, as presenter, is to share what you know with others. This type of presentation is a great way to showcase your skills, abilities, interests, and potential—depending on your audience. You're the expert, and this is your time to shine!

Keep Perspective

I have made the mistake of being so in love with my subject, with all its details and nuances, that I strayed from my purpose and my audience's needs. In a presentation on work/life balance, for example, I let the discussion venture into Maslow's Hierarchy of Needs—fascinating stuff to me as a psychologist. Yet my intended purpose had been to provide the members of my audience with five things they could do TODAY to add balance to their lives.

When you are an expert in your topic, your presentation's purpose often is to provide information, education, and training. You may also be called upon to present reports. Typically, your audience is interested in what you have to say because it benefits them in some way. You will need plenty of data, organized and prepared in ways that are meaningful for your audience, to support your presentation.

You Have Seniority or Experience

Sometimes you're tapped to make a presentation because you're the most senior person in your department, whether or not the presentation's topic falls within your area of expertise. A classic example is new employee orientation, in which a department member explains the department's functions and procedures to newly hired staff. Or you may find yourself presenting your department's productivity report to upper management, or the latest sales figures to the monthly division meeting.

There is a certain logic in this approach. As a senior member of your department, you have more experience in your department's procedures and likely the operations of your organization as a whole. You know people, processes, issues, and sensitivities. Your supervisor or manager may rely on you to take the lead in shaping the actions and work habits of other staff, and less experienced employees may look to you for guidance and answers. You may not know every little detail of your department's functions, but your knowledge level is quite high. People trust what you tell them.

You've Done It Before

Maybe you filled in for the boss at the monthly sales meeting or stepped in when the scheduled trainer came down with the flu. You did a good enough, and maybe even a stellar, job, and people praised you to the powers that be. Like it or not, you've become a featured presenter, a go-to person. This is a high compliment to you, and a great opportunity to hone your public speaking skills. Embrace it!

No One Else Can (or Will) Do It

Duty by default. Or, as your job description may say, "other responsibilities as assigned." That's what happens when your boss turns to you in a staff meeting and assigns the presentation to you. You may have little to qualify you for the assignment other than being in the line of sight. Your work is cut out for you, and there's plenty of it. To be honest, often there's not much glory or gratitude in these situations. Attendance at the presentation may be mandatory, establishing an audience reception that ranges from disinterest to outright distain.

Sometimes, however, presenter-by-default ends up having unexpected benefits for you. I often find that I learn a lot by giving a presentation. If the purpose is educational or informational, I might be doing research that I haven't done before, or taking the time to learn what is really behind my ideas or the tools that I use. I have a mission to deliver something useful to my audience, and I grow in the process.

When you're a reluctant designee, it may not be clear to you why the presentation is taking place. If you're unsure, ask. (This is good advice for any presentation, really.) And keep asking until you get the answers that will help you frame your presentation's foundation.

You Volunteered

A lot of people (like me) genuinely enjoy speaking to groups. You may have a natural ability to connect with people of diverse backgrounds and interests, or have such compelling enthusiasm for your topic that others can't help but at least listen if not become enthusiastic themselves. People who excel in marketing, sales, and customer service often do well in public speaking situations that require presentations that sell, motivate, or persuade. If you are such a person, your key challenge may be organizing and presenting material in a way that fulfills the needs of your audience (which chapter 2 covers).

WHY THIS PRESENTATION?

In the best of circumstances, the purpose of a presentation is clear-cut, such as to deliver the findings of a report or update skills. Other times the reason for the presentation is sketchy or is not what it appears. Unless your job is corporate trainer, you probably don't initiate presentations. Most often, someone requests you to give the presentation. That someone has a reason for wanting the presentation. Your mission is to find out.

The first fundamental is to answer the question: "Exactly what is the reason for this presentation, and what do I want my audience to take away when the presentation ends?" Are you presenting information or a report? Selling a service or product? Persuading a board of directors to fund your project? Motivating employees or volunteers? Teaching new skills? Your answer should be one brief sentence. This sentence is your objective—the purpose of your presentation. It is the seed. Plant it in fertile soil—your own passion—and nurture its growth with appropriate preparation, and it will blossom into an effective presentation.

OBJECTIVES AND EXPECTATIONS

Objectives are what you want your presentation to accomplish. Expectations are what the audience wants or needs from the presentation. In tandem, objectives and expectations are the starting point for your presentation. Your objectives and the audience's expectations should mesh with one another seamlessly.

Objectives and expectations are crucial to your presentation's design and delivery. Presentations flounder when you do not take the time to formulate, or ask for, clear objectives. This is one realm where less is more. For most presentations, three to five objectives are ideal.

The objectives help define the presentation's overall format. For example, if I am presenting the results of research, I keep in mind that the audience probably needs to know how the research was conducted, and how we answered their specific questions. I may also want to talk about additional findings. And I want them to know the questions that remain.

Though your purpose generally has the greatest influence on your objectives, your audience and your topic further shape and refine them. Chapter 2 talks more about meeting the expectations of your audience, both obvious and hidden. Chapter 3 discusses how to shape the content of your presentation to integrate your objectives.

Sometimes a presentation's objectives and expectations have multiple levels, depending on the purpose of the presentation. Others who may have objectives for and expectations of your presentation include stakeholders, such as corporate leadership. Make sure you know what your stakeholders expect of you as the presenter so you can accomplish this aspect of your purpose without overstepping your boundaries.

TYPES OF PRESENTATIONS

Presentations come in a variety of flavors, largely defined by their purpose. The main types of presentations are informational (which includes reports, education, and training), motivational, persuasive, and sales. The type of presentation often determines the tone and format of the presentation. Training presentations are often highly structured by the presenter, for example, while motivational presentations have wide latitude for the audience to shape the flow and direction. We'll come back to the different types of presentations in later chapters, when we get into research, preparation, challenges, and delivery.

INFORMATIONAL

You may be called on to research a topic, or to mine your own experience and expertise, and develop a presentation that is informative to your audience. This may be the complete presentation or it may be a piece of a presentation that has another overall purpose. I have been asked to provide an overview of qualitative research, a combination of basic theory and examples from my experiences. You might be asked to talk about a specific technology or a project methodology as the basis for a project your company has been assigned.

A presentation designed to impart information also might be used to describe a corporate decision or a reorganization or introduce employees to a new product, a new marketing strategy, or a new advertising campaign. A presentation with this purpose may require some of your own information gathering to make sure you have all the facts, and that you organize them logically and in a way that will be relevant to your audience. What does your audience want or need to know? What is the current level of knowledge? What gaps are you filling in? Once again we come back to objectives: It is critical to have clear objectives so that you are providing useful information and not going above or below the knowledge and interest levels of your audience.

The informative presentation:

- Fills in gaps in what the audience currently knows.
- Provides a basis for a decision or a new direction.
- Needs to feature details relevant to the overall purpose or goal.

As much as the information may interest you as the presenter (especially if you're an expert on the topic), adults only want to know what they need to know and what is relevant to their jobs or the corporation's expectations of them. Part of your presentation's structure should be a continuous reinforcement of this relevance. Bring every key point back to this, and you'll keep your audience's rapt attention.

Keep in mind that the informal communications machine within the organization may have been grinding out propaganda, much of it disseminated through e-mail or in the lunchroom, long before your presentation. This means that your audience may walk in feeling that they know more than you, know what you're going to say, or know what you are not telling them. You may feel like the audience collectively has a chip on its shoulder.

You may need to begin by dispelling myths and misinformation, relying on your own informal research or on what you know about how employees react to issues like new products, new marketing, and reorganizations. Other aspects of your purpose may include dispensing some motivation with the information, or doing a sales job about the benefits of the changes after you have given the news.

Subsets of informative presentations include reports, education, and training, which additionally have their specific and unique qualities.

Reports

As a researcher and consultant, I often am asked to present the results of some research I might have conducted on behalf of a company or organization. This is an opportunity to bring the research to life in ways that a written report can never do. It also lets my clients interact with me and ask questions about the research, its findings, and what it all means for them. You might find yourself presenting a report on your own research, on the progress or outcome of a project, on a product that you are developing, or on a marketing plan.

A report may present findings, results, conclusions, and/or recommendations, in isolation or in any combination. Your purpose may be only to present the recommendations, followed by the key findings that support the recommendations—the "do this and here's why" approach. Or your audience may need to hear an overview of the findings, supported by examples, to get them in a receptive mind-set—especially if the findings are unexpected or the recommendations are going against conventional wisdom. This is the "here's what we heard, now do this" approach. Or you may present the key findings without any recommendations at all, leaving that to your audience.

While it seems obvious that a presentation about a report should illuminate the report's findings and conclusions, all too often this point stretches into a gap between intent and result during the presentation. These elements are often crystal clear to the person presenting the report but foggy to the audience. Make sure your report presentation connects the findings to what the audience needs to know and to do about them. Obscurity makes it appear that you're hiding something.

Distinguish Your Presentation from the Report

What works in a written report will bore your audience to tears. Use a different approach for your presentation. Use real-world examples that demonstrate the relevance of the report's findings, conclusions, and recommendations. Examples are lively, expand your credibility, and keep the audience engaged. They make the audience feel that it was worthwhile to attend the presentation rather than simply reading the report themselves. Spice up your presentation with video and audio clips, quotes, and statistics from recognized experts, customers, and prospects. This moves you away from the format of the written report into a presentation that holds your audience's interest.

Education

In a certain sense, each and every presentation should somehow educate your audience, even if only about your expertise. Educating your audience means providing them with one or more nuggets of knowledge that will help them to understand their jobs better, see their objectives in a different way, and somehow broaden their perspectives. Education might also mean establishing a foundation or framework for the future.

An educational presentation is broad based, with the goal of imparting knowledge that each member of the audience can then apply to his or her own situation. An example might be a presentation about the cost savings and environmental impact of recycling, with each person then implementing the recycling efforts that are relevant to his or her circumstances and capabilities.

It's easy to lose touch with your purpose and objectives in an educational presentation because its boundaries can be so loose. I do a lot of presentations about stress management, which, as you know, is a very big topic. I've been known to go into great detail about how past experience creates false beliefs and irrational thinking that leads to irrational interpretations. See? I've lost you already! Audiences don't always want to be educated in such a way. They want to know the five things they can do today to make their lives more manageable. As questions arise during the presentation they may lead to teachable moments that allow me to bring in some theory. But for the most part, outside the academic setting people are not interested in knowledge for the sake of knowledge. Educational presentations need to speak to the current knowledge levels of the audience and move toward what the audience needs and wants to know.

Training

Training presentations focus on teaching or updating specific skills. Many jobs and professions have mandatory training requirements. The objectives are narrowly focused and measurable. Of course, the specifics vary according to the type of training you're doing. Some examples might be:

- Perform cardiopulmonary resuscitation (CPR).
- Create a spreadsheet.
- Prepare a sample design layout.
- Operate a forklift.
- Demonstrate the protocols for a meeting with clients or employees from another country or culture.

When you are able to do so, specify a minimum level of skill in the area in which you are providing training (core competency) as a prerequisite for attendance. This helps to assure that your audience has a core level of ability so you can stay on track with your objectives.

If you're doing a training presentation, odds are high that you're an expert on the subject. Your presentation likely includes segments of explanation, demonstration, practice, and evaluation. In many ways, training presentations are the easiest because the objectives and expectations are specific and clear. They are interactive and often exhilarating for you as the presenter.

When developing a training presentation, I often find it useful to start with the end point—what does the audience need to take from the presentation?—and work backward to the starting point. This helps me to organize information in logical, sequenced blocks, keeping it relevant to the needs of the audience. It also keeps me close enough to my objectives to identify any ambiguities before my audience does. I can ask for clarification as I'm developing the presentation. The answers to these questions are essential:

- What are the explicit objectives for the training? Is there enough time in the planned presentation to accomplish the objectives, or do you need multiple presentations?
- How will you measure the results of the training?
- Is the audience segmented appropriately for the training? Does the audience need to be subdivided, or the scope of the presentation narrowed?
- What is the current knowledge or skill level of the audience? Is this a technical, jargon-savvy group or a general audience?
- What does the audience want to DO with the training? Are they doers or managers?

The more narrowly you can define your objectives and your audience's needs, the more effective the training. I used to go out to companies and train them on database management. Often, the breadth of people in the class ranged from the computer-phobic people who didn't even want to turn the computer on, to computer jocks who came armed with questions, to managers who only wanted to know what they could expect their employees to be able to provide in terms of information and reports.

I often felt like I taught them all a few basic skills, leaving half of the class behind at some point, and leaving all of them frustrated. Some frustration is inevitable when, realistically, you can't break the class down into segments as much as you would like to. Public school teachers deal with this all of the time. However, to make the presentation as effective as possible, get clarification, and agreement, on the minimal skills that all attendees should bring to the training as well as learn from the training.

MOTIVATIONAL

Motivational presentations assume that your audience is already sold on the objectives or goals, but maybe not quite committed to meeting them. The role of the presenter is to remind them of these goals and the audience's commitment to them, to clarify any misunderstanding, and then to provide a pathway toward success. And to add inspiration. This can all be a challenge because the presenter has to be committed first, and be willing and able to demonstrate this commitment. Otherwise, the presentation is only words.

I sometimes go into companies to do presentations on specific topics. I might do a presentation on time management, for example. Employees may be interested in time management but not motivated to do anything about it. I might begin my presentation by asking them if they are motivated and why they are or why they are not. One reason they aren't motivated is that they don't know if they can manage their time or not. It sounds too hard, or they feel they don't have enough control. I would motivate them by showing them what a time managed person looks like and then break the steps down, I would show them where they can have control.

Early in my consulting career I had the dubious pleasure of doing a time management presentation for a group of customer service reps. I prepared a motivational presentation on taking a different perspective on life, setting priorities, getting involved in meaningful activities, learning to say no. I was motivated but my audience sat looking at me, stone-faced.

The Audience Factor

First, they were customer service reps, one of the most abused group of employees in any company. They had no control over their schedules and came to work every day to be beaten up by angry customers. Whatever resilience they had, a never ending rush of paperwork buried. They needed more than time management to motivate them. They were overburdened and burned out. They needed to have their jobs restructured, adequate time away from the phones, a career path out of customer support. The company was never going to do that, and they knew it. Too late, I knew it, too.

The audience plays a significant role in your decisions about how to design and structure your presentation. For the same content, a presentation to a handful of senior executives, a presentation to a group of professionals such as technicians or doctors, and a presentation to a group of other researchers or consultants all differ vastly from one another. Each group is attuned to its own agenda and perspective on the objectives.

From this experience I learned to ask some key questions from whomever is hiring me to talk about motivational topics such as time management. These questions include:

- What control over their work lives, including time, do members of the audience truly have?
- How much flexibility do they have to make changes if they are indeed motivated enough to make them?
- What barriers—of any kind—do they face?
- Just what do they need to be motivated to do?
- Do they want to be motivated? Are they interested in change?
- Am I motivating in the optimal direction?

Without these answers, the only possible outcome of the presentation is frustration for the audience and for the presenter. Even though this is not training, the audience needs to be taken by the hand—here is where you are right now, here is what you are getting and what you are not getting, here is here you could be and what it looks like, here is why it is possible, and here is what you can do to get started on realizing this vision. Don't overwhelm the audience with a vision that is way beyond where they are now without also showing them what steps they can take TODAY to move them closer or to reach it.

PERSUASIVE

Presentations intended to persuade may be focused on presenting a new idea or direction and getting the audience to at least consider it, if not embrace it. Comparison is a common tool in persuasive presentations, demonstrating to the audience why one option is better than others. Whereas with motivation you encourage members of the audience to find their own ways to apply your message, with persuasion you strive to direct the audience to apply your way (the way of the presentation) and only your way.

Three factors are crucial when you are making a persuasive presentation:

- You must have an in-depth understanding of the current approach so you are able to highlight what does and does not work about it.
- You must be able to present the new approach in light of how it is better than the status quo.
- You must be able to conclude with a vision of the future with the new approach.

Though persuasive presentations are similar to motivational presentations, with persuasive presentations your agenda is to sway the audience's thinking in a very specific direction—to choose a particular product, service, philosophy, or whatever.

SALES

Sales presentations often blend information, motivation, and persuasion with the specific goal of obtaining a decision at the presentation's end. Selling can involve a product or a service, which means presenting benefits and making sure the audience understands why this product or service is one that no one can live without. It means leading up to a crescendo in which the audience, or a key audience member, is asked to not only make a decision but to decide in the favor of whatever it is the presenter is offering. Sales can also mean "selling in" an idea, which often happens in agencies. In this way a sales presentation is similar to a persuasive presentation, only with a very specific decision as the goal.

Without patronizing the audience or compromising your credibility, you need to show the audience that they are missing something. An audience is measurably more receptive to a sales pitch that is geared to its specific situation. When I talk to people about sales approaches, the one complaint I hear the most is that salespeople have no experience or understanding of their industry and haven't done their homework.

Stay Positive

Talking down to your audience or talking trash about a competitor carries a steep price: your credibility. Instead, focus your efforts on making comparisons that highlight benefits and attributes—the upside of your product or service. Showcase your advantages and the disadvantages of the competition will reveal themselves.

Be interactive! Engage your audience. Don't tell people what they need. Instead, talk with them and help them to tell you what they need. Gain agreement. And then offer solutions. Show that your product or service is the best. At the end of a sales presentation, ask for the sale. Simple as this sounds, it's the step novice or inexperienced sales presenters forget or are reluctant to take. But more often than not, it's the final step that closes the sale.

Chapter 2

Your Audience

Your audience is the second leg of your presentation's foundation triangle, interlocking with your presentation's purpose (chapter 1) and your presentation's topic (chapter 3). Your audience is the "who" of your presentation, and their needs and expectations are crucial for appropriate selection of content, format, and style. You need to intimately understand what your audience already knows, what your audience needs to know, how your audience will use the information you provide in your presentation, and how to connect with your audience to meet their expectations and your objectives. Also coming into play is the "language" the group speaks. You can't speak in industry shorthand—jargon—to people who don't understand the industry, but to people who do, this both saves time and enhances your credibility.

Learn as much as possible about your potential audience. This knowledge will guide not only what you present but how you present it—the amenities you provide, the jokes you tell, the way you dress, and any special needs you have to accommodate. The composition of your audience influences your tone and style, too.

For a presentation about making healthcare decisions, for example, I may emphasize barriers that impede the decision-making process for an audience of healthcare professionals such as doctors, nurses, and social workers. My tone and demeanor would be authoritative and professional. For the same topic presented to an audience of patients or consumers, I'm likely to take a more touchy-feely approach that focuses on how emotions and lack of knowledge influence healthcare decisions. For either audience, I would also want to know what audience members need me to do—educate them about resources, offer suggestions, provide a roadmap of recommendations, or report on research findings.

You may find a mix of audience types in one presentation. For example, line employees and managers and even executives may need to attend the same information briefing. I have taught courses in introductory database searching to employees at all levels. What brings such audiences together is what they need to acquire from the presentation, not necessarily what they have in common with each other. Your mission, as the presenter, is to know your objectives and provide a presentation that hits just right across the spectrum of your audience. Otherwise, your presentation just hits in the middle somewhere and misses the mark with nearly everybody. One-size-fits-all is a myth, in clothing and in presentations.

THE VIEW FROM CENTER STAGE

Your audience may be there because of interest in the topic, or because attendance is required. Or the audience may not even be there at all, in the traditional sense, but instead be participating in the presentation via remote communication such as Internet or video conferencing, an increasingly common scenario in today's global community. Your audience may be your peers, your superiors, clients and customers, or people with no connection to you or to each other beyond their interest in the presentation.

As important as knowing who's in the audience is knowing why they're there. Are they interested in your topic, acquiring information that they in turn will present to others, in attendance because they are required to be there, looking for a way (*any* way), to get out of regular work for a few hours or a day? Each member of your audience has his or her own agenda that may or may not be apparent to you.

YOUR PEERS

Many people are more apprehensive about making presentations to audiences of their peers than to audiences of complete strangers. I am among them; to be honest, I find giving a presentation in front of my peers is the most stressful. There are a lot of reasons for that, some of them based on my own perceptions and baggage, and some of them just part of the deal when you present to people who are your equals. After all, what makes me so special that I should stand in front of them? Well, the truth of it is that any one of us could present to the others, and we'd all learn something!

I often work that much harder when I prepare a presentation for my peers—I make sure every "t" is crossed, every "i" is dotted. I think through all the possibilities: missing details, arguments that may come up, hard questions I may have to answer. When I step out there in front of my peers, I'm fully prepared. (Of course, this level of preparation really should go into *all* presentations.)

Part of this is pride. In presentations to most other audiences, I leave when the presentation is over. I don't interact with these people on a daily basis and indeed may never see many of them again. Any mistakes I make stay in the room, with no one to bring them back to confront me when I least expect it. And part of it is commitment to my team. These people, my peers, populate my daily world. They know at least something about my topic and may even know as much as I do. For this reason, it is especially important to understand the purpose of any presentation to peers—*why* it is that I am standing in front of them instead of sitting among them.

The Up-Side of Peer Audiences

Giving a presentation to your peers is a great way to get your ideas out there, to show your peers what you know, and to get their feedback. This type of presentation often feels more like an exchange of information and can be a gratifying experience. And when your own peers think you've done a good job on a presentation, then you probably have. You're not likely to garner any false praise from people you see every day.

When you're preparing your presentation, call some of your peers and ask them if they have any specific needs that you can make sure you include. If your peers feel that they've been included in the process, then they will be more likely to buy in and become a supportive audience. It can also be helpful to get advice from someone that your peers respect, such as a big name in the field or an executive, for additional credibility.

Give Credit Where Credit Is Due

You may want to begin your presentation with an introduction that references that you have obtained a lot of helpful feedback as you developed the presentation. Doing so demonstrates that you did not create it in a vacuum, and for your audience to rip it apart may mean ripping apart other colleagues as well. But be careful about naming who helped you, to make sure you don't offend people you did not ask.

If possible, ask one or two peers that you trust to review your presentation before you give it and provide feedback, including questions that they have. And if you can, practice giving your presentation to them. It's a great confidence builder that helps you feel more comfortable in front of your peers as well as prepare for the unexpected.

Construct and deliver your presentation in the language of your peers—this is one circumstance in which you can freely toss around buzzwords and industry shorthand. But don't show off in this regard; to do so is to invite criticism. Make sure you understand exactly what your peers know about your topic at this point in time as well as what they need to know (the purpose of your presentation). When you present information your peers already know, you risk boring them or appearing to be a lightweight who is barely up to date. On the flip side, when you leave gaps or your peers are not up to speed for your starting point, you risk making them feel stupid. It's often a good idea to start out with a review of the core concepts to get everyone on the same page.

Peer Audience Challenges

Issues and concerns can arise during presentations to peers that are not as likely to surface in presentations to other audiences. Among them are:

- Peers can sometimes have large egos (as can presenters). They can ask questions that may be in part aimed at catching you off guard so they can step in and try to show that they know more.
- Professional jealousies may come into play. Peers may feel that they should have had a greater role or that you have established yourself in a way that they have aspired to, which may result in some lack of receptiveness.

- A peer may be aware of recent developments that you are not aware of or may be aware of an aspect of your presentation, such as training or information, that you don't know about.
- It is difficult to be a prophet in your own country. If you are talking to people who have worked with you in the past, or who currently work with you, they may not consider what you have to say as worthy of their attention.

It is, of course, essential to keep your own ego in check. Focus on the topic and your goals and let the presentation fall into place around them. If you are focused entirely on projecting and protecting your own ego, you risk coming across as pompous and/or defensive, and those in your audience with their own ego agendas will be all over you before you know what's happening. The result is often an escalation of conflict when it doesn't need to be there.

Part of the Team

It is especially difficult to motivate or persuade your peers because they may not recognize you as a leader, or they may assume that you are trying to bully your way into a leadership role. If you find yourself facing this kind of resistance, shift your phrasing from "you" to "let's." Make it clear that you are part of the team and not trying to push them. Ironically, if you can persuade them to rally around you, then you will be more likely to be perceived as a leader.

If you do get dissent from a peer, or someone trying to show that he knows more, during your presentation, try to simply thank the person for the input and move on. One objective of such a challenge is to hijack the audience. It's counterproductive to take on the challenge in front of the group; to do so is to surrender the audience. There's more information about this and other audience challenges in chapter 9.

YOUR SUPERIORS

It can be scary to present in front of people who control your promotions and salary increases, who possibly know a lot more about the topic than you do, who have personalities that may be intimidating or hard to read, and who may or may not have time to listen to what you have to say. Your superiors, though likely to be more receptive than your peers, can be a formidable audience for you to face.

When I present to superiors I start to feel myself getting much shorter, as if I were regressing back to a child, with all that goes along with that. What if I mess up? What if they don't believe me, respect me, trust me, want to hear from me . . . like me! Of course, none (well, very little) of this is real. Nonetheless, the worries are there and can become a self-fulfilling prophecy if you fail to recognize them in time to head them off, as has happened to me on occasion.

When I worked in an ad agency, I had to present a project overview and a series of recommendations to a group that included peers and outside clients. That was stressful enough, but I felt ready. And then the head of the agency walked in about five minutes before we started. I had only met her once, and she was a very approachable person, but her appearance at my presentation caught me by surprise.

As I got underway, I felt myself stammering, hesitating to gather my thoughts, second-guessing myself. And when I finished I realized that I'd lost track of my purpose and my self-confidence. I also realized that I had given the presentation to her and her alone. I hadn't broken eye contact with her once during the presentation. The experience reminded me that I have to be grounded enough, secure in my material and in my purpose, so that I don't topple when I feel threatened.

You cannot know too much about your audience! Find out ahead of time who are the key individuals in attendance and what their personalities are like. Focus on the most important person in the room and make sure that his/her needs and expectations are accommodated. Most likely, all others in the room will take their cues from the MIP. Is this MIP bottom-line? In love with the details? Academic or topline in approach? Does this MIP stay only for the highlights and then walk out?

I try to get this information through my main contact, such as a client, or when I worked for companies, from my boss. With the permission of the main client, I have also talked informally with the administrative assistants of the key people who will be in attendance, just to make sure I am developing a presentation that will meet the MIP's needs and expectations.

If you are presenting a report, make sure you know whether recommendations are expected. Sometimes, key people want to make the recommendations and don't want to be told what to do. Other times, they expect the presenter to have thought through the information, project specs, report, and other details so as to have recommendations as well. Again, find out what is expected of you before you prepare your presentation.

The Up-Side of Presentations to Your Superiors

You gain a lot of important visibility when you present to superiors. You give yourself a chance to demonstrate your knowledge and your passion for the goals of the organization and for meeting the demands of the client and the market. When you give presentations to your superiors, you have a chance to have a real impact—they may ignore your e-mails or not come to the same meetings, but during that presentation they are your captives and you have their full attention.

The Challenge of Presentations to Your Superiors

If you are not grounded, then you also have a monumental opportunity to goof up, like I did during the ad agency presentation. And the blame can compound. Your bad performance can end up making your boss look bad. If you are an outside consultant, the internal client may also not look good if you don't come across well. And if your presentation has errors of accuracy or corporate politics, your superiors can be left with misperceptions that may be difficult to dispel. As an outside consultant, I am especially concerned about this. Sometimes outside consultants are given credibility they haven't earned, and their recommendations, even those that are ill conceived, can have major impact.

No Good Surprises

Don't catch anyone by surprise. Your presentation to superiors should be reviewed, sliced, diced, vetted . . . before you get in the door. When training superiors, be careful not to embarrass them in front of each other or in front of their underlings. Don't call on them in class or otherwise put them on the spot. Instead, leave pauses for questions or comments and let them jump in.

Make sure you are working closely with your peers, as well as your internal client if you are an outsider, or your manager if you are an insider. Get their input and their review. Make sure your presentation has been blessed, and that it contains no surprises. Surprises are always embarrassing to someone. Be authoritative and self-confident, but avoid coming across as too sure of yourself. This can be annoying at best, and threatening at worst.

Introduce your presentation by thanking your audience for the opportunity to be there. And thank your manager or the client who hired you—spread some of the credit around—this makes them look good and increases their visibility. They will, in turn, think more highly of you. And it reminds the audience that you are working in collaboration with other trusted people, so they know you are not a loose cannon.

SUBORDINATES

Being in a presenting role with subordinates can be a nice bonding experience. You are showing what you know, and enhancing your leadership relationship, as well as reminding them of why you are the boss (that would be, of course, because you know so much more than they do). When presenting to subordinates, you can be in the driver's seat in terms of the objectives. What do you want your audience to come away with? Are you providing them with needed background, a status update, motivating them, or training them? You really have the opportunity to shape the way that you want to be perceived, the kind of leader you want to be.

If you have an agenda with the company, keep it out of your presentation. Don't grind axes with your employees—don't make digs at company policies or executives you don't like. Employees may enjoy hearing this and agree with you, but at the same time you will lose respect and undermine your mission. And this always comes back to bite you later.

Speak to the level of your employees. This is not an opportunity to show off what you know. You are there to enhance them, not yourself. Be careful about calling on employees. It can be very stressful to be called upon by your boss during a presentation. They will feel on the spot and embarrassed. And if another employee jumps in and answers the question, they will be even more embarrassed. Instead, provide the employees with various opportunities to ask questions of you.

The Up-Side of Presentations to Subordinates

Presenting to subordinates is an opportunity to enhance your relationship with them but also opens the door to alienating them through a poorly planned or executed presentation. When I worked in a corporate setting I used to enjoy giving presentations to my team. It was a chance to get them together, to present them with information that they needed to know, and to interact with them.

But when I became a manager, these presentations struck fear in my heart in some of the same way that presenting to superiors did. What if I look stupid? What if one of my employees calls me on something I said, or challenges me? What if that employee knows more than I do? What if I send them all off in the wrong direction? These worries led to insecurity that came through in the presentation. I appeared unsure of myself and overly concerned about the opinions of my audience. It took me some time to overcome my insecurities.

Challenges of Presentations to Subordinates

You may feel as if you are on the spot and being judged in terms of your competence as a leader. When I worked in the computer industry, I managed employees who were more technically knowledgeable than I was. This was a concern for me in group situations. I had to present updates or information and I could not necessarily answer all of their questions from a technical perspective. And some employees had a techno jock attitude that caused them to want to challenge me at times or to question why I was managing them. This was just an attitude in the industry. I learned to make it clear what my role was as a manager and why I was presenting information. I learned to collaborate with employees and ask them to contribute where they had expertise that I did not have. I would talk to these employees ahead of time and let them know where I would need them to support me. This showed respect for their knowledge and got buy in from them.

Other challenges during presentations to subordinates may include:

- An employee may attempt to show off by grandstanding in front of other employees.
- You may have a passive-aggressive employee who wants to challenge you.
- Employees may be afraid to ask questions for fear they will look stupid in front of their peers, so you may leave them lost but not know it.

You can increase the sense of buy-in if you talk to employees individually before your presentation. What do they need to know, from how they see things? Use the presentation as an opportunity to enhance the team. Give them small exercises that make use of the material and provide an opportunity for them to work together and report back—for example, get together again to make recommendations, or strategize on what that will mean in terms of their specific functions and roles. In addition to providing an opportunity to interact, it will also provide input that you may need.

WILLING PARTICIPANTS

You can't ask for anything more than an audience full of people who want to be there. When people want to attend the presentation, it is much easier to work with them. They are anticipating the information and are automatically involved. But willing participants may also expect a lot. Their willingness may not be realistic. They may be expecting more than you are planning to deliver, or more than you can deliver. They may be expecting a presentation at a different level, or with a different focus.

Again, knowing what the audience wants and needs before the fact will help a lot. You can make sure you are meeting their expectations or, if not, you may have the opportunity to let them know that your objectives may differ from their expectations.

I always start a presentation with an agenda that includes a list of topics. I also go over my objectives. I may even ask audience members, if it is a small group, to briefly tell me their expectations. In any event, I want to make sure my willing participants are in sync with where the presentation is going before I begin.

MANDATORY ATTENDANCE

I do a lot of presentations through employee assistance programs. Sometimes the audience is voluntary, and often, as a result of that, small. Other times, the audience is mandatory, but also larger. In a law firm, for example, if it is not mandatory, only administrative assistants and mailroom employees come because the attorneys are worried about getting all of their billable hours completed. If the presentation is mandatory, the room may fill but two thirds of those who are there clearly don't want to be—and they show it.

I did a presentation on respect in the workplace at a small pharmaceutical lab with technicians from other countries. Attendance was mandatory. The lab's manager requested the presentation because the technicians were getting together in groups and speaking native languages when the rule was only to speak in English. Other factors were also in play that had created tension. I complimented them on being very welcoming and helpful when I had arrived—numerous people had offered to help me find my way to the presentation room. I made a joke about how easily I get lost. And then I told them I was happy to be there even if they might not be happy to sit through my presentation. When all the cards are on the table, it's easier to move forward.

Meeting the Resistance

I have a technique I call meeting the resistance. I say to the group, "I know you are required to be here. Let's not pretend otherwise. And I know some or all of you have an issue with that." Generally I see some responsiveness, even if it is just rolling eyes. Then I make some kind of joke about not shooting the messenger. This often helps to loosen them up. I add that I really understand this, and that the last thing I want to do is to bore or frustrate them. I then say I will do my utmost to provide a useful experience. If possible, I ask for their input on what I can talk about that might be relevant.

In some ways, a mandatory attendance presentation can be a worthwhile experience. It guarantees that anyone who can benefit from the presentation, or who needs to be, will actually be there. For the presenter, the rule about knowing the needs of your audience and preparing ahead is critical. Given the resistance, it is important that you quickly get to the points that the audience most needs to know. They are not going to be patient while you flounder around, or bore them with extraneous detail.

Invite your audience to ask questions or to express concerns. Again, meeting the resistance means being willing to deal with that resistance throughout the presentation.

If the presentation is motivational, I might even go as far as to say that I have met with a few of them (if I really have) and gotten some kind of understanding of the resistance. I might add why I understand how they feel and relate a similar experience. Again, this will help break things down. It isn't any fun resisting someone who isn't playing their part in the game.

REMOTE

Increasingly, I give presentations through videoconferencing or video streaming. It is important to understand the technology. For example, the observers often experience a delay between what they hear and what they see on the screen. If, during the presentation, we are attempting to interact, we cannot talk over the top of each other. One person needs to finish talking before another person begins. I have to anticipate when someone is about to talk and let them start and finish before I jump in. This can get annoying if it is not handled carefully, so it is to your advantage to work with the technician to make sure you know how the technology functions.

Your Onscreen Image

Keep in mind that no one looks great on video without makeup and it adds twenty pounds to your figure. Don't get distracted if you see yourself on screen.

Organizations that frequently use technology for presentations usually have an established etiquette for interaction during the presentation. I once addressed a law firm in New York City on their employee assistance program benefits. Four other offices were involved in other parts of the country. I asked how I should handle the Q&A. I was informed that each office had a team leader who would funnel the questions. I provided pauses frequently so that someone could jump in with a question or a comment.

If you are using visual aids such as PowerPoint slides projected, these may not be visible to the people who are receiving the presentation via videoconferencing. So don't assume your remote audience can see such items—ask them what they can see. If your remote audience cannot see what is being projected on the slides, explain the visuals and refer to them as little as possible. Also ask if your presentation can be distributed in hardcopy to remote audiences before the presentation begins so that they can follow along. Take care to speak clearly and ask if everyone "out there in TV land" can hear you.

SPECIAL NEEDS

Virtually every audience I address has a special need in some way. Sometimes food is involved, and I need to make sure we have accommodated vegetarian, kosher, non-beef eaters, and so on. In other circumstances, you need to accommodate disabilities such as visual impairment, hearing impairment, and physical mobility limitations. Most U.S. locations where you might give presentations are required by federal law to be accessible to those who have disabilities.

Before you begin your presentation, ask any audience members who have disabilities what will make the presentation easier or more useful for them. You might take care to describe what you write on flip charts or other visual aids when you have someone who is visually impaired, for example.

A diverse group may include people of different nationalities who speak languages other than English, so you'd want to arrange for translators. Often the presentation's organizers do this but it's a good idea for you to cover this base, too. When I do research, this may be conducted in other countries. If people from the United States are involved, I get translators. I also make sure that if they are eating, their dietary preferences are accommodated.

STAKEHOLDERS AND HIDDEN AUDIENCES

A stakeholder is any person or entity that has a vested interest in your presentation. This might be a client who hires you to conduct presentations within the organization, or the organization's board of directors or shareholders. These same entities may also be a hidden audience for your presentation, not in attendance but fully aware of the presentation's content and the audience who is there.

The Man in the Moon Test

When I teach, I tell my students to give their assignments the man in the moon test before turning them in. I say, if the man on the moon landed on earth and he was handed your paper, or your presentation, and he knew nothing about the topic, would he be able to read your paper and walk away with some understanding of what you were trying to say? If he only knew correct spellings, and couldn't understand typos, would be confused by misspellings? This same "test" also applies to presentations. If the man in the moon were seated in the audience, would he understand?

When I address an audience that includes stakeholders, I make sure that I clarify that I am an outsider, and not a member of the organization who is sponsoring the presentation, such as my client. But the audience does not hear that. They view me as an extension of the sponsor, as a spokesperson for the sponsor even if I am not, even as employee of the sponsor no matter how many times I tell them that I am not. They just assume that if I am there, I have been vetted by the sponsor.

I consider this to be an honor and a major responsibility. I am careful how I conduct myself. I watch my humor. I make sure I am not saying anything that may be perceived as representing my client in a negative way. This also applies to hidden audiences. In fact, I assume this is always a possibility and that there is someone watching (and even present) that I don't know about. And if shareholders are involved, I make sure that the executive of the company has signed off, or at least I try to push for this. No one—least of all the presenter—benefits from nasty surprises.

When giving a presentation where stakeholders are present, the presenter really needs to be buttoned up. This includes putting forth a professional appearance and making sure you look your best. It is a good idea to make sure that your PowerPoint slides have been carefully reviewed for content and format/spelling, both by someone who is a good proofreader and by someone within the company. Not only for look and feel, but to make sure you are not saying anything that could be misunderstood.

A caution: companies sometimes want to be placed in their best light where stakeholders are concerned, and your internal client at the company may also want himself or herself, or the department, to be placed in the best light as well. I sometimes encounter this when I am presenting research, for example. It is not that I am being asked to tell barefaced lies. But sometimes I am asked to "soften" certain findings or not discuss my recommendations. This can be a tricky situation because you obviously want to work cooperatively with your client, but your professional integrity cannot be placed at risk in any situation, even if this is not intended.

When such a situation comes up, you will need to finesse it with your primary contact. Work to find a middle ground that doesn't leave you feeling as though your integrity has been compromised.

Chapter 3

Your Topic

The third leg of the triangle that forms your presentation's foundation is your topic—the subject of your presentation and, from the audience's perspective, the reason for your presentation. It would seem that choosing your topic is a no-brainer. You may have volunteered or been invited to speak on a specific topic. Or the whole thing may have been dropped in your lap. But I have learned that no matter how straightforward things appear, there is the topic and then there is the TOPIC.

Let me step back and admit that I love psychology and psychological theory and just talking about these issues. When my enthusiasm consumes me, I tend to assume that other people feel the same. I often do presentations on work-life balance. I have a basic outline that includes what it means and doesn't mean to have work-life balance, what lack of balance causes in terms of stress and lack of productivity, and some things to consider when attempting to achieve balance.

On one such presentation, I really went to town on this topic. Maybe someone from the audience asked me a question that set me off, maybe it was just one of those days when there was no containing my joy for my work. I was full stride in my element. I talked about why we really can't define work-life balance and how it is really an individual matter. I talked about why as a culture we have such high expectations about balance, that we need to be superproductive and superconnected to our families and communities, but that work productivity always wins out. I talked about the emotional and physical toll that being out of balance can cause.

I LOVED this presentation. I was starting to feel like Tony Robbins in my own meager way. During the final five minutes (all the time I'd allotted for questions), I asked people in the audience—which was comprised mainly of women, some of whom were mothers and some of whom were single—what they did to achieve balance.

One of them started to talk about limiting her children to three seasons of sports and then one season off so that she could take a break from carpools and uniforms for a few months. Another chimed in about scheduling her social events to make sure she didn't work too much.

Interesting, I said. Sorry, we're out of time.

Did I cover my topic? Absolutely. Did I cover the topic in the eyes of my audience? Nope.

One of the women came up to me afterwards and admitted that what she really needed and hoped to get from my presentation was, "five things I can do to get more balance in my life."

"Can you tell me that?" she asked.

I rattled off five quick ideas.

"Next time, that's how you should start the presentation," she said. "That's what we needed to know."

So there you have it. The topic and the TOPIC.

You should be saying, "But you could've prevented this situation by following your own suggestions and processes from chapters 1 and 2!" Award yourself five brownie points. You're right. I easily could've provided exactly what this audience needed had I put the appropriate effort into defining my purpose and my audience. I slipped into the mistake that my depth of knowledge about my topic was all I needed to dazzle this audience. Unfortunately, what I gave them was the dazzle of rhinestones rather than the shine of diamonds.

AUDIENCE KNOWLEDGE ABOUT YOUR TOPIC

You can't speak to the specific needs of everyone in the audience, at least not on any level of depth. But you can certainly get an idea of what they currently know and then use that as a starting point. I often begin presentations with a review, just to make sure everyone understands the foundation I'm building from and has a vision of where the presentation will go.

How do I learn what the audience already knows about the topic? I talk to whomever is my main contact for setting up the presentation. I try to make that person responsible for bringing me up to speed. Depending on the purpose and type of presentation (education, training, information, and so on), I ask:

- What is the audience going to do with the information they acquire from the presentation? What do they need to walk out with?
- What have they been doing/how have they been thinking so far? What is their current orientation to the topic? This may range from clueless to having the basics but needing some gaps filled in to just needing an update and a fresh perspective.
- What mistakes/errors/pitfalls/challenges have they been facing? This will provide me with some insights into where the gaps may lie. My contact cannot always articulate where the audience is at this point but even that is useful information for me.
- Why does the audience want me to talk to them? This will also provide additional insight.

• Is there someone I need to talk to for additional perspective on the topic as it relates to either the audience
or the presentation's purpose? Your contact may not
want you talking to anyone else, out of concern that
you may contribute to the perception that he or she
lacks competence, but it is worth a try.

Keep in mind that your contact may not understand the
audience's current knowledge level, so direct questions may
not be as revealing as you'd like. Consider scheduling a meeting with your contact and a few key members of the audience,
or a spokesperson for the audience, to make sure you have the
appropriate perspective while keeping your contact involved
(the politics of it).

Ask for examples—what members of the audience know,
how they use their knowledge, what efforts are effective, the
gaps or the need. The more specific the example, the more useful. Again, this is an indirect way of understanding where your
audience is in terms of knowledge, and should provide you
with some direction that will help you to make the presentation more relevant.

I can't emphasize enough the importance of gearing the
presentation toward your audience, as much as you possibly
can. The audience will quickly turn you off if they feel like you
are talking below them or above them.

YOUR KNOWLEDGE ABOUT YOUR TOPIC

You must know your topic. If you don't, you're going to step
into a very deep hole. Your audience will know that you don't
know—it's not something you can hide, especially from the
stage. Audiences smell blood when the presenter stammers,

looks off into the distance, hesitates, backtracks . . . and there is always someone who will lunge to the attack and will call you on it.

I start a presentation by telling the audience what I am going to tell them, my role—why I have been asked to be the presenter—and what I can address and what I won't be addressing. I tell them my understanding of why I am there. (For discussion on the presentation's purpose, see chapter 1.)

I also make sure I am prepared to handle every detail of my presentation. If it is on PowerPoint, I go through every page, and every bullet point, and ask myself, "Why did I include this information?" I make sure I can answer that, which may require me to do further research. And if I can't answer the why, I ask myself whether that item needs to be in the presentation at all. What is it adding?

Knowledge does not just mean theory. Depending on the presentation, you may need a lot or a little bit of that. Knowledge also means arming yourself with practical experiences and applications, because this how your audience will apply the information you provide in your presentation. Double-check your facts and details each time you use them in a presentation, to make sure you are up-to-the-second. Little will sink your credibility as quickly as outdated information.

I find that depth of knowledge about the topic contributes greatly to my comfort level in giving the presentation. Knowledge is power. When I feel knowledgeable about my topic, this gives me confidence and enthusiasm that can catch like wildfire with the audience. They can't help but respond. Knowledge produces a passion that can't be ignored. Not only that, but I'm a terrible liar. If I am not comfortable with something, from the perspective of knowledge, it will quickly be obvious to the audience. I don't want to stand in front of a group and feel incompetent.

So I don't handle topics that are outside my knowledge zone. For example, I am not going to go into an organization and talk about eldercare laws even though I am comfortable talking about the issues that go along with taking care of elderly parents, such as the emotional and logistical factors. But law is a stretch for me—a big one. No amount of research is going to make me a credible speaker on matters of the law.

This is not to say that you should never venture beyond your comfort zone. You'll never grow, and soon enough you'll be as bored as your audiences. And you may have little choice, if you find yourself delegated to do a presentation on an unfamiliar topic. When possible, choose areas to expand into that relate to your areas of existing expertise or aptitude (natural abilities) and build your knowledge base from a solid foundation.

RESEARCH

There are many ways to do research; one is not necessarily better than another. What's important is that if you need to do it, you do it, and you use the resources that are available to you. For most of my research these days, I've forsaken the public library in favor of the Web. I Google everything, even the topics I am familiar with. I want to make sure I am considering alternate perspectives, new developments, and other factors. I love books, but the Internet is right there, 24-7. In a few keystrokes, I can tap into the resources of nearly any library in the world. And wireless access means I even can use my notebook computer during a break in a presentation to confirm a fact or check something the audience brings up.

What is important to keep in mind is that the Web is the world's largest vanity press. Anyone who has anything to say can say it on the Web—no fact-checking, vetting, or peer-review. You don't always know the credentials of the person whose article, Web site, or blog you're reading. Are these "experts" any more qualified than you are? Are they grinding an ax of some kind or playing out a hidden agenda?

The Library Is Still a Valuable Resource

For the record, I haven't totally given up on the library. It can be a great place to peruse journals or recent magazines, even just for background information. Because printed materials require more effort to produce, there's a natural process of screening. However, it's still important to use multiple sources.

Healthy Skepticism

Always be a skeptic when you are using the Web. Check and double-check credentials, and exercise great caution believing credentials. Remember that what appears to be an original posting often is not, even on Web sites noted for their reliability. For most research, you're better off to stay with the Web sites of universities and established research organizations. Many commercial Web sites are also good, though it's hard for you to know whether there's a slant to the material that favors the corporation presenting the information.

To the extent possible, go to multiple sources for information. Finding the same information on multiple Web sites is no guarantee of its accuracy; content is often licensed to multiple users and commonly plagiarized (a discussion of copyright and other legal matters appears later in this chapter). When you use in your presentation ideas and concepts that originated with someone else, have the source information with you. Tell your audience that you've done your research, and this is what you learned and from whom. Let them help decide the credibility as well.

Another facet of knowing your audience (the second leg of your presentation's foundation, see chapter 2) is knowing what experts the audience trusts and respects. Who are the thought leaders in their field? Bill Gates? Billy Graham? Bill Clinton? Research what these thought leaders have to say. I also call people who are experts or who can connect me with credible sources, both published and in person.

Research Formats, Styles, and Approaches

Research is not only for information itself but also for how to present information. I've taught counseling and psychology courses that included a brief discussion of statistical analysis. I don't enjoy numbers and this is not an especially comfortable topic for me. But it is a necessary component. So this is an area where I do a lot of research. Not only on the details—I know this information—but on alternative approaches to present the material.

For example, I understand standard deviation but I have trouble explaining it. It doesn't roll off my tongue the way it needs to in front of a group. So I got on the Internet and searched on "standard deviation," and then on "teaching standard deviation." I was able to access back lectures from other college professors in which they included a component on standard deviation. One of the lectures did this by using standard deviation to explain sports scores. Now, I don't know much about sports, either, so I certainly wouldn't step up to the plate, so to speak, with that approach. But reading this lecture did give me some ideas about how to explain standard deviation through a fun example, and I was able to take it from there.

I also research group exercises that I can use, if that is a part of the presentation. Brief little things I can have the audience do to liven things up, for example, introduce themselves to the person sitting next to them, and then asking that person to remember three details about what they just heard. I have purchased a number of books that include exercises of various sorts, and I often look through them for ideas.

I also may ask my contact to provide me with information that gives me a feel for what the audience knows, their needs and concerns—particularly white papers, articles, and books. This can be really helpful because it can offer insight into their attitude, and the language they use. I don't necessarily want to go in spouting their buzzwords but I do try to at least be familiar.

DETAILS AND FACTS

Too much detail can put the audience to sleep, and isn't needed, as much as I might love those details and facts. As I have said in previous chapters, know your audience and what they need to know and speak to that. This sounds simple but at least for me, it is very easy to think you know where you need to go in the presentation and the level it needs to be, but then when you get deep into your presentation preparations you lose sight and get caught in the forest. Use as much detail and fact as the presentation requires—only what is relevant and useful.

Including facts in the actual presentation can add credibility and interest. If I am talking about reactions to medical diagnoses, for example, I might begin with some basic statistics about the numbers of people being diagnosed every year with a condition such as diabetes, assuming I am going to reference diabetes later in the presentation. This helps create the focus. This fact will come from a recognized source, and it is like having an expert stop in and say, "this is an important topic and you should listen to this guy."

You may choose to keep certain details and facts for your own use, as background or to draw upon if questions come up. Often, I store such background details and facts in a Word document, double spaced, with subheads and bullet points, so if a question or discussion arises and I need this information, I can quickly draw upon it. I don't assume that I will remember anything, especially if I need to get to something quickly, or if I am being challenged. I prepare myself with a lot of background.

Know Your Sources

Know that every time you present any kind of information—timelines, research results, background information, training—you may need to present your sources. I once used the phrase, "the political is personal," or something like that. I think it is a great phrase. I admitted that I hadn't made it up when I used it. Someone asked me where it came from and I said I didn't know. Someone else raised her hand and informed the audience that a well-known feminist had made this statement. This was not a big deal within the group and I had at least been very upfront that the phrase was not mine. But I had used a quote and could not attribute its source.

In the case of report presentation, such as a project update, this kind of detail might include when the project was commissioned, when it started, the major high points in the time line, what was due at each step of the way. Invariably, this will come up and I want to have something to reference if it does.

If I am providing information, such as background on a research project or even an employee assistance presentation on a topic like stress or time management, I like to have background detail beyond the depth of my planned presentation. If someone wants to ask a question, say, about the biochemistry of stress, I want to be able to access that information to adequately answer the question.

For topics that are not in my usual repertoire but that I might be called upon to talk about from time to time, I keep

Word documents updated with subtopics, facts, and details. By doing this, I avoid the need to reinvent the wheel every time I give a presentation. I am familiar with these documents, and so locating a specific topic is not difficult.

When I present research findings, I make sure I am totally prepared to answer questions that arise, and they certainly do arise. I might address how the research was conducted, what kinds of people were interviewed, where and when the interviews occurred. Invariably someone will ask a question about how I found the people to interview, or want to know some detail about the backgrounds of these people. I can't include all such details in the presentation because the presentation would be too unwieldy, but I can certainly make sure I have the information I need to answer such questions.

BUZZWORDS AND JARGON

Buzzwords can add credibility to your presentation when they are appropriate for your audience (see the discussion of this in chapter 2). However, a little goes a long way. If you load your presentation with buzzwords you risk alienating your audience, which may perceive you as a phony. This is especially a concern when you're not part of the audience's industry—you may misuse a buzzword, use jargon not everyone understands, or you use buzzwords that are outdated.

There is nothing worse, in a presentation of technical content, than being called upon to define a buzzword that you have just used only to realize that you are not quite familiar with it. In addressing audiences with a technical background, I used to go overboard in tossing out acronyms because I had picked them up from earlier discussions. But when an audience member, or two, wanted then to take that discussion further—because by using that word I had created the impression of technical knowledge that I did not have or because someone just felt like challenging me—I learned to pull back on buzzwords.

It can be helpful to toss out one or two buzzwords, assuming you are totally familiar with them, just to let the audience know you've done your homework, but nothing beyond that. There are too many landmines you can step on in buzzword territory.

ANECDOTES AND STORIES

Anecdotes and stories bring presentations to life. They add dimension and perspective to your content, giving your audience a broader context for the information. I pull anecdotes and stories from my own background (as I am doing in this book) and I pull them from other people, carefully recounted and diligently referenced. Even if you are not very experienced, you can do the same. Pay attention to what people say and do, in your workplace as well as in your presentations. Before long, one or two stories becomes a cache of dozens from which you can choose.

Protecting Privacy

As fascinating as are stories and anecdotes, no one likes to think he or she could be the star story at your next presentation. It's essential to protect the identity and privacy of individuals, companies, and even circumstances. An effective way to do this is to create composites from multiple, similar situations. Such creative liberty does not distract from the power and value of the anecdote and allows you to tailor details to target a particular audience.

The reaction to a personal story is visceral. I can see my audience immediately perk up when I say I have a story to tell them. For example, I teach graduate counseling students. When I am doing a lecture, the moment I signal that I am going to talk about one of my own counseling clients (within the appropriate safeguards to protect identity and privacy, of course), I can see that I have everyone's focused attention. So I intersperse anecdotes and stories throughout the presentation. I have the audience's interest and attention during the story, and then they stay with me for at least awhile after that.

I choose anecdotes and stories that bring certain aspects of the information to life or illuminate theories. This keeps the fun stuff on track with the presentation's objectives. Even if the discussion digresses, I can easily bring it full circle back to the point I was making. In a training presentation, anecdotes and stories can be really useful in terms of illustrating how to use the information or skills. When I taught database management, I would give examples of how key clients were using the system (with the client's identity protected, of course). This worked well because the members of the audience could relate to the experiences of other companies. They would realize that if other companies were using it in certain ways, so could they. This gave them encouragement.

When presenting research findings, stories are invaluable. When I am talking about a key finding, I'll add a story. "For example, one doctor I talked to said. . . ." Or, "One patient experienced. . . ." Everyone in the audience sits up a little straighter. It's magical!

I sometimes recount stories or anecdotes I read elsewhere. When you do this, you must take care about accuracy and attribution. There may be someone in the audience who has heard the story differently. And no "telling tales out of school." Confidentiality is crucial. You might want to use an anecdote or story from a famous person, or from a person who is recognized in the field that is represented within your audience. An anecdote about a key researcher in a medical institution or university, or an anecdote about a well-known person such as Bill Gates, can add interest and credibility to any presentation.

COPYRIGHT MATTERS

Copyright is the legal protection granted to the author of original material that affirms the author's ownership of the material. There are many ins and outs to copyright but the bottom line is that if someone else wrote it, you need permission to use it—often even if you credit the material's source and author. Many, many well-known experts, researchers, and writers have been caught using material that should have been attributed to someone else. The list is long and highly distinguished—and embarrassing. It's not a list you want to join.

Plagiarism

Using someone else's material without appropriate credit or permission is plagiarism and can land you—and your organization or company—in legal hot water. Copyright laws in the United States are fairly stringent and provide extensive definition of what uses are permitted. Copyright laws in other countries may differ. When in doubt, get permission—in writing.

There's nothing wrong with using someone else's findings, ideas, or statements as long as you make it clear exactly what is coming from someone else and specifically attribute it to that person or entity. Using the name and institution or book title in the presentation is fine, but always have the additional details with you in case someone has a question during the presentation or afterwards.

When you use someone else's material and ideas, make sure you do so in the original context. Don't use parts of things, such as quotes, to illustrate a point that the original author did not intend or in a way that distorts the intention. This is dishonest. And someone in the audience will know and your credibility will fly out the window. Not to mention that you could find yourself in the proverbial heap of trouble from a legal perspective.

If you provide a hardcopy of your presentation to audience members, make sure that you include a reference section with all of the details about each source you use. There are many resource books and guidelines that tell you what information to include and how to present it. Be especially wary of material you draw from Web sites on the Internet. Many, even some that are structured as reference sites, do not properly cite their sources. It is important to identify the *original* sources of material you use in your presentation.

Chapter 4

Developing Your Presentation

You remember I told you in the Introduction that building your presentation was a process of assembling three triangles? Chapters 1, 2, and 3 covered the first triangle: your foundation of purpose, audience, and topic. Chapters 4, 5, and 6 cover the second triangle: the stages of your presentation's development. We'll start with a short quiz to help you identify your presentation style, then dive into the nuts and bolts of building your presentation.

WHAT'S YOUR STYLE? A QUIZ

Take a few minutes to answer the following questions. Select the answer that best represents your response.

1. In my mind, another term for a presentation is:

A. A conversation among friends.
B. Words of advice from an experienced peer.
C. A lesson from an expert that leaves me awestruck.

2. The use of music during a presentation could:

    A. Help the audience feel more relaxed.

    B. Add some "flavor" to the presentation.

    C. Only be useful if the composer was being discussed.

3. Note-taking during the presentation is best handled through:

    A. Audience members can take notes if they desire.

    B. A summary outline would help audience members to organize their notes.

    C. Presenter should provide a detailed outline so audience doesn't have to take notes.

4. A presenter who does not allow questions until after the presentation is:

    A. Overly authoritative.

    B. Trying to stay within time limits.

    C. Focused on keeping the presentation on course.

5. During a presentation, the flip chart may:

    A. Potentially be a distraction from the flow of the discussion.

    B. Be helpful in keeping track of comments from the audience.

    C. Be kept off to the side to help reinforce key points.

6. If audience members do not offer comments or ask questions:

    A. The presenter is falling flat on his/her face.

    B. The presenter may need to make sure audience members feel comfortable in speaking out.

    C. The presenter has clearly done a thorough job.

7. Extensive practice before the presentation:

A. Should not be necessary if the presenter knows the subject well.
B. Is necessary so that the presenter appears comfortable and engaging.
C. Is essential to assure that each word of the presentation is appropriate.

8. The presenter's notes should look like:

A. A list of topics.
B. An outline with topics and key points.
C. A speech.

9. The use of video during a presentation might include:

A. Movie clips that could serve to raise the energy in the room.
B. Movie clips that are relevant to key points in the presentation.
C. Video clips that are specific to the topic but nothing beyond that.

10. If an audience asked me a question I couldn't answer, I would:

A. Assume this is part of the collaborative experience.
B. Remind myself that I couldn't have anticipated every question.
C. Be surprised that I could have been this careless in my preparation.

Count the number of As, Bs, and Cs that you circled. If you primarily circled:

As, your style is laidback and casual.

"A" Strengths

- Your presentation will be fun and engaging, like a graduate seminar conducted at a local bar.
- Your presentation will feel self-directed and relevant to the audience.
- Your audience feels engaged and embraced and bonds with you.

"A" Weaknesses

- You may be led off topic such that audience members enjoy the experience but afterwards feel like they didn't learn anything.
- Dominant audience members may define the agenda.
- If audience members are expecting a lecture or more content, they may refuse to participate.
- You may feel prepared until you get in the room and then flounder.

Bs, your style is semiformal and interactive.

"B" Strengths

- You have adequate content to fill the time.
- You leave room to adjust the presentation (if the scope and time allows) to the needs of your audience.

"B" Weaknesses

- You may go off topic.
- If you are not totally comfortable, you can lose control of the presentation.
- Some audience members may expect a more formal presentation and be disappointed.

- You may have an audience that for some reason is not comfortable interacting.

Cs, your style is formal.

"C" Strengths
- Not one word is lost during the presentation because you have made sure of that.
- You have declared yourself the expert and, with this credibility, audience members will be more receptive.

"C" Weaknesses
- Audience has minimal chance to interact with you; they may not have a chance to get clarification on a key point and you won't know.
- Audience may leave confused and not enlightened.

Good presenters are able to combine some or all of these elements into any given presentation, based on their comfort level with the audience and their experience. When you are a new presenter, you may want to be more formal (a "C"). It is always a good idea to be over- rather than underprepared. What is most important is to meet your objectives, even if you are not as engaging and welcoming as you would like to be when you first begin presenting. Better to be slightly "wooden" than ineffective and unprepared. A semiformal and interactive (a "B") presenter is more likely to be viewed as effective.

We are not always provided with total flexibility when we present. Some topics require a more formal approach—a motivational speech versus a eulogy—and whoever is asking us to present may have some preferences as well.

YOUR COMFORT ZONE

As you may have learned in the quiz, each of us has a comfort zone when we do presentations. This includes the basic styles that we covered in the quiz as well as your comfort with your ability to present the material.

Some of the most knowledgeable people are also terrible presenters because they don't know how to translate the material from what they know, or do instinctively, with the needs of the audience. Sometimes people with less expertise but a grasp of the theory and practice are much better presenters. Obviously, the level of the audience is a factor here, for example, a layperson audience versus an audience of advanced practitioners.

Make sure your starting point is the material itself—what you know and need to be able to know, and what your audience knows. If you're feeling any discomfort at all in terms of your ability to talk about your subject in a way that is relevant and enlightening to the audience, ask yourself why. Do you need more practice? Is there a missing link in terms of what is intuitive to you but not to the audience, and can you cross that bridge to make sure they understand each step?

Let me come back to my statistics example here. I don't use statistics much but what I do know has become somewhat intuitive over the years. I know about standard deviation, for example, because I live somewhat in that world. But explaining standard deviation to someone who doesn't understand the concept is a challenge. When I need to provide this explanation in a presentation, I practice it over and over.

Sometimes I talk about topics that are bound by confidentiality. For example, I may be doing an update on research findings. In such situations, I may know details and information about my client's corporate strategy that some of the audience members do not know. Before I sit down to start the presentation,

I make sure that I totally understand what I should cover and what should not be discussed. This is also part of my comfort zone.

While your presentation style is an important element of the comfort zone, keep in mind that we may be asked to stretch as presenters. I have learned to conduct brainstorming sessions, which are completely unstructured. This has taken a lot of training and practice on my part. I am comfortable lecturing—and love it—but totally unstructured brainstorming requires the ability to control yet not appear in control, to keep things on track while also letting the discussion meander within very specific limits. This has been a stretch for me—and pushed me way beyond my comfort zone—but has made me a more flexible and effective presenter. I have even been able to include some of these brainstorming skills and methods in more formal presentations.

LOGICAL PROGRESSION

If you don't know where you want to end up, you're going to have a tough time finding your way there. Through the years I've done my share of floundering—out of my own creation—during the process of trying to put a presentation together. And this was in part because I didn't know what I really wanted to say. But just like a road trip, you figure out where you want to go and start from where you are.

The overall framework I, and many other presenters, use is the classic "tell them what you're going to tell them, tell them, and then tell them what you told them." Remember freshman English? This is your introduction, content, and conclusion. (Yet another triangle.) This simple yet effective template guides the development of the flow of presentation as well as the materials. The structure applies no matter what the format of your presentation, from notes you follow yourself to multimedia or PowerPoint presentations.

Introduction: Tell Them What You're Going to Tell Them

Your introduction establishes your purpose for giving the presentation and lets the audience know what you intend for them to get from the presentation—objectives and expectations. Most presentations have at least two objectives and no more than five, unless the presentation extends over several sessions. In such a circumstance, each session should have its own subset of objectives.

Your introduction may also establish, with more or less formality depending on the nature of the presentation, the basic knowledge level you expect the audience to have. Training presentations in particular often require a prerequisite level of skill. Your introduction should comprise about 10 percent of your overall presentation.

Content: Tell Them

The content segment of your presentation is the reason you—and your audience—are here. This is the "meat" of your presentation. Organize your content in a linear fashion that makes sense for the material and the audience. That is, concepts and information should flow. Present material in manageable "bites" of information. This is a bit vague, I realize, but the size of the bite varies with the material and the audience. Sometimes you need to adjust the pace—how fast you present the bites—after your presentation is underway, if the audience is either ahead or behind where you anticipated.

Keep it short and simple—another tried and true guideline. Your support materials (handouts, visuals, even multimedia presentations) should provide key or summary points. You are the presenter; it's your job to actually present the material. Are you using PowerPoint slides? Use bullets, descriptive words, and short phrases to structure information "bites." Build from one concept or thought to the other in a progression that makes sense from the audience's perspective.

The amount of information in each "bite" must be manageable. These guidelines will help you structure your information:

- Use an odd number of points (one, three, five, seven).
- Have no more than seven points (three to five is better).
- Use simple phrases that are three to seven words in length.

This is how the brain most efficiently and effectively processes information. Each piece builds on the next to create the overall structure you want to provide for your audience. This approach is as useful for you as it is for your audience. I don't always think very logically, particularly when I'm talking about something that is second nature for me. Or I may be very familiar with one aspect of a process and want to focus there, but not provide enough background for my audience. Logical organization of my material helps me stay on track.

Conclusion: Tell Them What You Told Them

Your presentation's conclusion summarizes the key learning points or objectives. I sometimes prepare my conclusion, especially for informational presentations, by repeating my objectives and pairing each with the achievement. For example, in a presentation about dealing with difficult people I might have as one of my objectives, "Learn three methods for separating a disruptive person from his or her audience." In my conclusion, I would summarize this and pair the point with the methods I covered in the presentation:

Three Audience Separation Techniques
1. Stand up or step in front.
2. Step away from and behind.
3. Pen and notepad.

Such a summary reinforces the key messages of your presentation by requiring the person to connect the "bites" with the more extensive information you provided during your presentation.

TIME AND ENVIRONMENT

I once did a presentation at a company on time management. I arrived (on time) and asked for my contact. She met me at the front desk, and we walked to the room where the presentation was to take place. She opened the door to a beautiful, well lit training room. However, there was a small group currently using the room. One of the members of the group turned to her and said, "We will be here for awhile."

She turned to me with a sheepish grin and informed me that the executive committee of the company was using the room and we would need to find an alternative. Well, we did. It was windowless, overheated, and too small for the group who showed up. They were angry at having to give up the training room for this tiny, cramped room. As a result, they were not responsive to me or to what I had to tell them. Some of the audience was outwardly hostile. And here I was trying to tell them how to be more productive!

Afterward, I told my contact, an HR manager, that we should have canceled the program. Not only had it been less than useful, but it had actually been an experience that eroded morale. Environment cannot be underemphasized. The room needs to be well lit, the chairs comfortable, with an adequate writing space if needed, and comfortable heating or air-conditioning. To ignore the environment is to risk—even invite—failure.

The presenter needs to advocate for the audience. Don't ask me to conduct training when the audience does not have a flat surface to hold their training materials and take notes. Don't ask me to brainstorm and break into small groups when we are packed into auditorium style seating that cannot be moved around.

Not that I can't be flexible. I am flexible in terms of modifying my presentation to the environment, but not in using a format that does not fit the room. If there is no place to spread out, we don't break into small groups. I might ask audience members to talk briefly with the person sitting next to them, for example.

Time is also a key consideration. Adult attention spans are not infinite. In fact, they are not any better, and sometimes are worse, than the attention spans of children. Adults need a mix of lecture and interaction along with a break every hour to stretch and refresh themselves. I am careful about what happens directly after lunch. People get sleepy as their food is digesting. So midafternoon, I build in some interaction.

I am also careful about what happens first thing in the morning. The audience may need some time to wake up, so I try to give them some moving around and interaction time if it is early morning, so that people who are wide awake and people who are still clearing out the cob webs all have a chance to get on an equal footing.

MEDIA OPTIONS

Choosing the media options begins with asking what is available. Don't plan a multimedia extravaganza for an organization that only has an overhead projector. On the other hand, don't bring overheads to a high flying high tech company.

We live in a multimedia world. And when we present, if we can address more than one of the five senses, we can be that much more effective. We keep our audience more involved, the information will be that much more relevant, and people have different strengths. Some learn better when they read text, others when they see pictures, still others when they hear something. But if you can hit at least two of the senses you are that much further ahead.

I often teach in a classroom that is outfitted with a large multimedia deck that allows me to play CDs, DVDs, project a magazine article, and go on the Internet. This room delivers a subtle message to me as an instructor: we don't expect you just to come here and lecture and neither do your students.

When I do research projects, such as focus groups or interviews, my clients sometimes use clips from the research. We videotape, with the permission of the people being interviewed and with their permission to use the clips for internal purposes. And then we go through the clips—a very tedious process—to pull quotes that support key findings.

It is instructive for me to tell the audience, for example, that elderly people often have to make hard decisions about whether they can pay for drug prescriptions. But when I say this, and then show a clip in which an older woman tells the story about how she decided to stay sick for an additional week rather than pay for an antibiotic, the audience really gets my point. They may not remember what I said. But they will replay that clip over and over in their minds, and hopefully be motivated to take action.

This approach works well in a broad range of presentation types, bringing a multimedia spin to the concepts of stories and anecdotes. You also can draw from public sources (though be cautious about copyright—see chapter 3). I was teaching about intelligence testing. A few days before that I read an article in the newspaper about how people who are told they are smart may actually behave in a more intelligent manner. I cut this article out and projected it to the class. Seeing it added credibility to my discussion and provided a visual distraction from looking at me (not that I am not great to look at).

You have probably been to a conference where the opening session included music and some kind of visual stimulation such as a slideshow or video. Most likely, you were that much more engaged. Multimedia presentations also engage the emotions in ways that a speaker may not be able to. And when learning or information is associated with an emotion, it is that much more likely to be remembered. What do you think advertisers have been doing for decades through television and radio broadcasts? Think of the old AT&T commercials. Was it the availability of long distance that you remember, or the young child reaching out and touching grandma?

Using media doesn't have to be overwhelming. It can be a lot of fun, especially when you see how pumped up your audience gets over your presentation. Talk to people in your organization who can help you. You may have a department that works with media. If not, HR may have some resources, or the sales department. Or ask around and you may run across a frustrated auteur who will jump at the chance to help you out with some sound or video or even movie clips for your presentation. You might even carry around a digital camera or video cam and take pictures or clips for use in your presentation. (Again, keep in mind privacy issues.)

In any event, always consider the use of PowerPoint. It is not difficult to put together a simple PowerPoint presentation, even just enough to keep your main talking points projected while you talk. This provides some visual stimulation for the audience and helps them to stay focused on the major points you want to bring up.

Don't let the idea of PowerPoint overwhelm you. Microsoft has provided a great help system that guides you along the way.

And there is always somebody in your company or a friend who can help you out. There are many books on using PowerPoint, from the basics to the elaborate. If you are presenting on a regular basis, it would behoove you to take a class. And if you have kids at home, see if you can talk one of them into sitting down and guiding poor Mom or Dad through the process of creating their very first PowerPoint presentation. There are other multimedia computer applications, too.

I was very resistant to using PowerPoint at first. I had used an earlier version and found it hard to use to the point of frustration. And guys don't ask for driving directions and we don't ask for PowerPoint directions. Finally, I was working for an ad agency. I arrived back home at midnight from a client visit. When I arrived at the office the next day, at 9 A.M., I was informed that I needed to do a briefing at noon. PowerPoint required. I learned that putting together a basic presentation was not the hardest thing in the world. I also learned that co-workers can be called upon to bail out a neophyte.

HANDOUTS

Handouts are a mixed bag. Sometimes I use them and sometimes I don't. The decision has much to do with the mix of purpose, audience, and topic (that all-important first triangle). On the down side, the audience may focus on the handout and not listen to the speaker. Worse yet, audience members may read ahead in the presentation, decide there is something more interesting further on, and start asking questions ahead of time.

On the other hand, there can be value in providing an outline that the audience can use to follow along. It also provides an effective way for people to take notes. A more formal variation of the handout is the training manual, which is especially useful in training presentations where the presentation highlights and illustrates key points from the manual.

In an ideal world, I would not provide a handout for use during the presentation to help assure that I have the full attention of the audience. And then provide them with a "take-away" at the end of the presentation. That is what I usually do. However, I make exceptions.

When I am covering a topic like stress reduction, I might include both highlights of the presentation as well as exercises to complete. I take a break in my talk, for example, and ask the audience to make a list of stressful situations that they often face, or a list of how they react. In this way, the handout is useful in supporting the content and keeping the audience involved.

Also, consider who is in your audience. If I am presenting to executives, not only do I need a handout, for use during or after the presentation, but it probably needs to be in full color. And maybe even bound, so it looks nice. If the situation is more casual, I will be less likely to do something in full color, but I do at least provide a take-away.

Keep in mind that your handout is your legacy. Your audience may remember you or not. But your handout most likely has your name on it. So make sure it is typo free, totally clear, and professionally formatted and reproduced.

I also use my handout as a branding opportunity. I include my name, my company name, and my contact information. So if two years from now, someone looks at the presentation and asks, "who is this brilliant guy?" they won't have to struggle to find the answer.

If you are using PowerPoint, you have instant access to a handout. You can simply print your presentation in handout format, even two or more slides to a page. This can be useful to provide audience members during the presentation or as a take-away.

Sometimes I first create a detailed PowerPoint presentation that will be used during my presentation. And then I edit the original version down into a version that is the key topic and points, but not so detailed. I may use the second version as the handout.

VISUALS

Your presentation will be much more effective and memorable if you include a visual component. The days of standing at a podium and only talking are over. Handouts, slides, Power-Point, video clips, movie clips . . . all of these will help keep your audience more involved and your presentation moving.

Don't forget that your audience members are spending hours sitting in front of computer screens in full color, sneaking in and out of the Internet where everything is in full color. Kids are playing videogames and using the computer at schools and at home. We live in a multimedia world and we can't expect people to settle for a speech just because, as speakers, we don't want to take the time to pull in visual support and don't see why we should have to be entertainers. You're right. We don't have time and we shouldn't have to be entertainers. But we do have to include a visual component and we have to find the time or risk looking like, and being, a dinosaur. And we all know what happened to the dinosaurs. . . .

YOUR NOTES

I love the idea of being totally spontaneous. With some presentations, like stress management, I can be. At least I think I could be. But I have learned not to risk it. So I work from very detailed notes.

Sometimes, if I am nervous or didn't eat right the night before or that morning, or some combination, I can temporarily lose my place. If I am jet-lagged, I am guaranteed to lose my place, at least temporarily. If I am distracted by an unexpected question . . . yes, I can lose my place.

If I am using PowerPoint, I print out a full page version of each of my PowerPoint pages. And then I include notes on each page. This helps me to be reassured that I am going to remember to bring in each of my key points. The notes are in red. And it helps to assure that if I momentarily lose my place, I can pick up where I left off.

I may still have a page of notes, in Word, for each Power-Point page. I just make sure the page numbers in the Word document correspond with the page numbers in the Power-Point presentation. I do this when I am presenting something with a lot of detail, or if it is a presentation that I have not given previously. I don't write it as a speech because I don't want to end up reading it. It is easy to get lost in a paragraph and have to keep finding yourself.

My notes might look something like this:

Key Symptoms of Stress

> **Cognitive**—*loss of short-term memory, difficulty in concentrating*
> **Behavioral**—*blowing up in anger, bursting into tears*
> **Emotional**—*anxiety, panic*

This is enough to keep me on track because I know my subject. I just need to be reminded of the key points I want to emphasize.

I might also include references to examples that I want to provide, such as:

> **Example**—*a guy gets a flat tire on the way to an important business meeting. Has to decide what to do next but may be so stressed out that problem solving abilities are impaired.*

These notes will trigger the rest of my story. But if I am distracted or momentarily unable to think clearly, those key points, or that example, may temporarily elude me.

Notes Cannot Overcome Lack of Preparation

Your notes are not an excuse for not preparing adequately. And detailed notes will not make up for lack of preparation. Notes are your touch pads; they guide your presentation.

Most likely, you will develop your own style for note taking for presentations. Until then, include enough detail to adequately support your practice sessions. Practice looking away, and then finding your place again. I use a lot of headings and subheadings, with incomplete sentences in bullet point format, and lots of white space so that I don't get lost. I also underline key words in red.

ANTICIPATING QUESTIONS AND CHALLENGES

I try to anticipate every possible question. Partly because I don't want my credibility to be compromised and partly because I want to walk away knowing that the audience is fully informed in a way that is relevant to their needs and expectations.

I use a variety of methods. I go through my presentation and give it the journalism test: Who, what, where, when, why. I also give it the man in the moon test (see chapter 3), with the hope that I can inform the totally uninformed. I might ask someone not involved in the topic to look over my presentation and see if anything is unclear—transitions, terminology, sentence structure. I include additional detail in my notes, or in a separate document, to have something to refer to if additional clarification is necessary.

I try to be hard on myself as I do this. Even if something seems like a pain, I make sure I am prepared with additional detail. What I remind myself is that I need to be the expert. The audience is coming to me because I know more than they do, at least regarding this specific topic, and I need to deliver on that assumption.

I learned this the hard way. I conducted a discussion with a group of technology experts regarding their perceptions of where a specific technology is going. I was the facilitator and was there to keep them talking, get consensus, and then, later, to report back to my clients. Fine. I have not billed myself as a technology expert and didn't see any reason to be.

However, the technology experts had used some buzzwords that were not familiar to me and, as it turned out, could be interpreted in more than one way. I hadn't bothered to learn the definitions of these terms, or to at least look them up. Guess what? Someone asked me to define a word. And then, when I admitted I didn't know (and ALWAYS admit when you don't know rather than saying something that may not be truthful), I asked if someone in the audience was familiar with the word. Two people were. Unfortunately, each offered a different, and potentially valid, definition. My credibility went out the window. And worse yet, the audience left with an unanswered question that was important to them.

On the other hand, I was reporting on a project that was focused on patient decision making. I carefully prepared the presentation—the who, what, where, when, why test, and so on. And then I decided to get some additional background so I put on my research hat, went to the Web, and looked up research regarding patient decision making, as well as the various decision-making processes in general. I came really armed with a lot of knowledge.

This knowledge added depth to my presentation. The background ended up sneaking its way into the discussion: "I have also read. . . . " The audience knew that they were not only hearing from one expert but from other experts as well. I was that much more confident. And the audience knew it.

There is always going to be someone who asks a question you can't answer. There is usually going to be someone who wants to challenge your credibility. Often, this is the same person. We will talk more about those folks in chapter 9.

Chapter 5

Preparing Yourself

Okay, you've prepared your presentation. The slides are done, the handouts are printed, your notes are ready. Now it's time to turn the eye of preparation on you. This is the second leg of the preparation triangle. How will you say what you've got to say—practically as well as emotively? How will you connect with your audience? What will you wear? What will you do to establish your credibility? Going into the home stretch, the focus of preparation shifts from the presentation to the presenter.

YOU'RE THE EXPERT!

When you stand in front of your audience and see all those faces staring expectantly up at you, you may have a sudden urge to flee. After all, what do you know to be in this position? Relax. No one knows everything, and most adults not only recognize but are pretty comfortable with this. After all, it takes us all off the hook!

So when you step in front of that audience, they don't expect you to know everything. They only expect you to provide for them the information they came to receive. Each person in the room knows more than you do about *something*. But you have something they want, too. In their eyes, you are the expert—whether or not you feel like one. You are more of an expert than you realize, when it comes down to it. Whether you volunteered or were delegated to do the presentation, other people have faith in your abilities. You should, too.

When I was a corporate trainer, I was not always the expert in what I was teaching, especially when I first started teaching it. Sometimes the material included technical content that I was familiar with (at best) but not competent in. I knew I was going to get questions. There was a side of me that wanted to wing it. I'm good at thinking on my feet. I can probably figure out a response to a hard question that will at least pacify the questioner. Or, I can refer the questioner to an expert who can answer the question.

Thinking I could think on my feet was a rationalization to justify my own resistance to really preparing to deliver the course. And assuming that I could call in an expert was self-defeating at best. But I tried it anyway. And guess what? I stumbled before anyone had a question. While delivering the material, I detected holes in my knowledge that I hadn't realized before. And then when I started getting questions . . . let's just say that by that point there was no recovery for me.

I learned the hard way that I have to be the expert about what I am presenting that my audience expects me to be, and to *really* be that person. This comes from preparation and through rehearsal, as I will talk about in chapter 6.

Unless you are a really good liar, though, if you don't really feel like an expert in what you are presenting, the audience will detect that. We all have ways of behaving when we are not truly comfortable with what we are saying, and subconsciously, your audience will pick up on those signs. So keep reminding yourself: you are the expert.

I use a lot of self talk. I tell myself that I am the presenter because I am the best person for the job. I am the expert (once

I have decided that by virtue of knowledge, experience, credentials, and preparation, I really am). This would seem obvious but self-doubt can creep in, especially when you are a relatively new presenter.

Sometimes, our own insecurities can become a nasty critic who beats us up for not knowing enough, for faking our expertise, for being in the right place at the right time but not because of our personal attributes, or for being designated presenter because no one else wanted the job (not that this doesn't happen at times).

But part of my preparation is to make sure that my self-talk is positive. Not only do I tell myself that I am the best person for the job but also that presenting is an exciting opportunity, a personal growth experience. And I tell myself that every time I present, I become an even better presenter. And you know what? I do! Such self-talk becomes a self-fulfilling prophecy—much better to focus on where you want to go than on what you fear might go wrong. Practice this with yourself.

ATTIRE

The question of what to wear is more than rhetoric at the closet door. There isn't really an absolute standard of dress for presenters. In general you can't go wrong wearing a business suit, whether you're a man or a woman. But it's also important to feel comfortable and confident in the clothes you're wearing—to dress in a way that "suits" you (pardon the pun). Feeling comfortable about your appearance is an important ingredient in doing a good job. You have to be yourself when you are up there on the podium.

I am not someone who loves wearing suits. I don't even *like* suits. In my perfect world, I would wear a sweater and jeans every day. I even wear light cotton sweaters in the summer.

If I have to dress up, a sport coat and a shirt, maybe with a tie, if I must, is okay. However, I have learned the hard way that I have to think very carefully about how I am going to dress.

We live in a world of snap judgments, and as the cliché goes, you don't get a second chance to make a first impression. When you see someone with a lot of tattoos, what do you assume? Someone in a tux? Someone in a torn tee shirt? We'd all like to say that we don't make judgments about others based on appearance, but we all do. It's because we're human. Nature has hardwired us to assess our surroundings and we have finely tuned that skill.

I have used some rationalization to justify my desire to dress casual. I have told myself that since I am a Ph.D., the rumpled professor look is okay. Or that if I look too formal, the audience will not relax. None of this rationalization is entirely true. What I have learned is the audience needs to perceive you as having a connection to them in some way. At the same time, they need to be able to look up to you.

You can move light years in establishing yourself by wearing the right clothes and projecting the appropriate appearance. Who is your audience? Executives and managers who wear Brooks Brothers for work? Then you also need to wear Brooks Brothers or comparable attire. Your audience judges you on this point, as unfair as it is.

They're Watching You!

I once gave a presentation for which I wore a suit. One of the audience members came up to me and informed me that the stripes on my tie were slanted in the wrong direction. Fortunately, for both of us, I didn't give him the response I would most have liked, but the experience did teach me that the audience is watching every last detail before I even open my mouth.

If the audience dresses business casual, you will also want to carefully consider how you dress. Business casual is an interesting minefield that can mean anything from jeans and sweaters (my idea of business casual!) to slacks or skirt and collared shirt or blouse.

But remember the credibility factor. Your business casual audience doesn't necessarily want you to be business casual, too. Audience members likely know each other and respect each other's knowledge and expertise, but they know nothing about you. If your dress is casual, your audience may not take you seriously—or worse, may think you don't take *them* seriously.

On the other end of the spectrum, I do a lot of presentations at a large technology company. If I showed up in a tie, they would think that I was stiff, pompous, and not serious in the same way they are serious about technology. So for these audiences I wear khakis and a button down shirt, which is a "dressy" version of their own office casual (many of them show up in tee shirts and shorts).

This company is based on the West coast and I am on the East coast so there is a regional issue here as well. They don't want some New Yorker coming out there and attempting to talk down to them, so it is important that I look like an equal. Regional differences are an important consideration. People in cities dress in a more sophisticated manner. I often find that in cities like Atlanta and Dallas, for example, people dress in an extremely sophisticated manner. I don't try to outdo them, but I make sure I am going to be acceptable. In smaller towns, people can be put off by someone wearing designer clothes.

What is the purpose of your presentation? This is another important factor to consider when considering the day's wardrobe. For a workshop or brainstorming session, I want the audience to know we're going to have fun together. So I want them to dress casually. But I may arrive wearing a shirt, tie, and jacket (and, of course, nice slacks) and take off my tie and loosen my collar at the beginning of the presentation. This lets my audience know I'm an "expert" because I look like I am but also that I intend to relax with them.

When in Doubt, Ask What You Should Wear

Generally I have a key contact who is arranging the presentation. I ask them what they would prefer me to wear, or I ask what other presenters have worn. This at least provides me with some valuable input, though I may still raise my own standard a notch or two to make sure I am not dressed down too much.

Be careful about colors and seasons. Choose conservative over fluorescent. In semicasual clothes, choose darker colors in the winter and lighter colors in the summer. I once sat in a presentation given by a very smart and entertaining woman who just happened to be wearing a hot pink suit. And it was late fall. I found my mind constantly drifting to that hot pink suit and how inappropriate it was. Another presenter wore a good suit but the pants were too short. So I ended up focusing on that suit and wondering why he was this unsophisticated or if he couldn't afford anything better. Maybe he wasn't all that successful. And I attended a technical presentation by a woman wearing huge spherical earrings that bobbed every time she moved her head. After a while, that was all I could see.

The bottom line: always dress in a manner that is subdued and respectable, and that will not in any way draw undo attention to you.

DEMEANOR

Ever watch a presenter who seemed to want to be a vaude-ville comic? Or who was so somber you wondered when the pallbearers were going to arrive? Or who seemed to have no personality at all and seemed to be reading from a script? Your demeanor has a lot to do with how a presentation is received. It is important that your demeanor matches the presentation, the topic, and the audience.

Consider your demeanor in context of the presentation itself. For example, if I am presenting research results or recommendations, then my tone is one with some gravity. That signals the audience to take what I have to say, and me, seriously. If I laughed and joked all the way through it, they wouldn't give any of what I was saying much credibility. If I am conducting a brainstorming session, or talking about something like stress management, I am more casual in my behavior. I make jokes, usually about myself, or about people with whom I have come into contact over the years. I might tell funny stories. This helps to loosen people up.

I have taught caregivers how to better communicate with the people they are caring for. When I do that, my demeanor is relaxed but also serious. I might encourage the audience to see the humorous side, mainly through showing the humor in my own experiences, but my demeanor is caring and concerned, not jocular. And being somber in this situation might cause audience members to shut down.

I sat in on a presentation on a drug treatment center. The leader of the seminar was a salesperson and not a mental health professional. His demeanor was that of a salesperson—upbeat, solicitous. He spoke to us as someone who was selling his organization's services but he did not have the caring and professional manner of someone who is involved in the actual treatment side. I felt like I was being "sold" and this made me uncomfortable. I would rather he had been less polished, even like a mental health professional who is not accustomed to public speaking, than have such a slick demeanor. (Going back to our earlier discussion about dressing appropriately for the audience, his expensive suit was also incongruous with the flannel shirts and jeans many of the drug counselors were wearing.)

All people need to feel like they are being respected. And one of the ways a speaker can show respect is by speaking to the audience in a respectful manner. In chapter 3, I suggested identifying the most important person in the audience; that works in the context of determining your demeanor, too. As I mentioned in chapter 3, most of the other audience members are going to follow that person's lead anyway. Organizational culture and diversity are other important factors.

Remember the high tech company I talked about earlier that dresses casual and expects the same from me? An early lesson with that group was that casual goes only as far as dress with that group. They are INTENSE. They are serious and focused from the time the presentation starts to the time it stops. They aren't interested in jokes—they are all business.

When I'm doing a presentation for this group, I sometimes think to myself, why all the seriousness? This is computer software. We're not curing cancer. And ironically, the professionals at a cancer center that I work with appreciate a more relaxed atmosphere and even see the humorous side to what they are doing. On the other hand, some of the highly polished corporate audiences may expect a somewhat relaxed demeanor. Sometimes they just want an outsider to break up the seriousness of the environment. Or they associate being somewhat casual with being self-confident and assertive. A large part of demeanor is common sense. Be too stiff, people wonder why you're so uncomfortable. Act too relaxed, they wonder what you're hiding.

Mind Your Manners

Language has become very casual these days. Slang and profanity are abundant. Avoid slipping to this level of casualness during a presentation. No matter how comfortable you feel, maintain professionalism in the way you speak.

I did several presentations to a group at a financial services company. The people in the group were always friendly, even laid back. This caused me to let my guard down by assuming that this was the corporate culture. I watched as they gathered, about fifteen of them, for one of my presentations. They were very relaxed—until one man walked in.

Suddenly the energy of the whole room changed. They nodded toward him but no one smiled anymore. People sat up straight in their seats and took out paper and pen to take notes. I said to myself: "I can't be laid back in this presentation or I will fail." Fortunately, I was experienced enough to modify my demeanor, though I have to say it was jarring to me to have to change so radically just when I was about to get started.

After my presentation was finished, the man got up and walked out. As soon as the door closed behind him, the audience visibly relaxed. After the presentation my contact at the company came to me and said, "He is a managing director visiting our office for a week. We didn't know he was going to show up. I hope he didn't freak you out as much as he does us."

BE YOURSELF

Sometimes the people who teach us valuable lessons do not do it in a very nice way, or in a way that we would most want. But they teach us nonetheless. I once had a manager pull me aside and in no uncertain terms tell me that I appeared uncomfortable and unprepared. She said I became a big man with a very tiny voice and that made the audience disconnect from me. She had no shortage of observations: I seemed to put up a wall around myself that kept the audience from connecting with me, she said. I was, in her eyes, ineffective.

I said to her: "But I don't know how to relate to these people. I don't know what they want from me or how to win their respect."

She answered, "People respect people who are themselves, who are comfortable with who they are, and who don't make any apologies for who they are."

It took a few years for that to sink in. After all, I was working with some high flying clients and I didn't view myself as their equal. But I looked around at other people who were making presentations, and they certainly didn't fit the image of a corporate executive. Some were academic, some were flamboyant, but all had something to say and said it appropriately, but in their own way. When I started to work with myself, instead of against myself, my presenting became a lot more powerful.

First, that was one less thing I needed to worry about. After all, it takes a lot of energy to try to turn yourself inside out to meet what you assume are someone else's expectations. And I started having more fun.

With experience, I have figured out who I am as a speaker. For example, I am not Robin Williams or Billy Crystal, so I don't try to be too funny. A little self-effacing humor gets a laugh, if I want to be humorous, and it relaxes the audience. But I am also not superserious, and if I go too far in this direction, I don't look real either. I'm most comfortable using my hands a lot, so I allow myself to gesture. I'm a Midwesterner at heart and have regional mannerisms that might contrast with someone from the East Coast or the South or another region of the country.

These details I have learned about myself. The more presentations you do, the more of these details you will identify about yourself. What those details are doesn't so much matter. Whatever our differences, we can all be equally effective.

PRACTICE, PRACTICE, PRACTICE

When I first started presenting, I made myself stand up and give the presentation word for word, and to practice it this way. Since I don't have a podium in my apartment, I stood in my kitchen, with the book propped up on my stove, while I addressed the air vent. It seemed silly, but I knew that if I didn't go through it word for word, I would miss something that was uncomfortable for me, or that I didn't understand as well as I thought I did.

That is a strange thing about doing presentations. Details that you thought you knew and understood, when you were reading through them, may seem anything but understandable when you actually have to present them to someone else. You suddenly see those little tiny gaps in your knowledge that are going to feel like very big gaps when you are trying to explain them to someone else.

I've found myself in the middle of a practice session only to suddenly realize that I don't actually know how to get from Point A to Point B. How does that happen, after all? This often comes up during research. We may be building a study on previous findings. But then we also looked in some new directions. Why did we decide to do that? What hadn't we learned previously? This gap may not be obvious to me when I am putting the presentation together. But when I am talking about it—telling the story of the research—I may suddenly realize that a piece of the story is missing. That little piece would be a glaring hole to my clients, and inevitably one of them would ask for clarification.

When you are first doing presentations, a lot of issues require your attention—your own emotions, reading the audience, keeping a grasp on the content, monitoring your pace, adjusting your demeanor . . . the list goes on. Sometimes all of these peripheral issues—like the stuffy managing director who has suddenly entered the room—can really throw you off base. You have to be conscious enough to take this in and decide how you are going to handle it.

The peripheral issues can really throw you off or at least temporarily draw you up short.

You have no control over this. But you do have control over how prepared you are to deliver your material. You can have it so ingrained, so second nature, that the core of your presentation stays constant even when nothing else about it does. And you can do this by really practicing. Over and over and over. . . .

I have different ways I do this. I might:

- Pick up my presentation and just skim through it when I have a few minutes, just to help hardwire the overall structure into my brain, including the major topics and the transitions.
- Focus on a section of the presentation that is especially touchy, just to give myself some extra practice.
- Focus on one section at a time, in depth, during those moments when I have only a small amount of time, practicing it mentally or, if I'm alone, saying it out loud.

But there is nothing like practicing a presentation from start to finish, multiple times. This ingrains the presentation in your consciousness so that the presentation will want to continue on its own when distractions threaten to derail it. If this is a presentation I give often, I might practice by pulling it out and reading through it, maybe adding some detail or examples that will be more relevant to my audience.

If it is a onetime presentation, such as presenting some research findings or making a series of recommendations, I remind myself that I only have one shot to do this right, but that the memory of me, and what I said, will linger afterwards. This is enough to motivate me to put in some extra time practicing.

Is there someone you can draft to listen to your presentation? A friend or a partner may sometimes help here. Ask your draftee to jot down observations, comments, and questions during your presentation so there are no interruptions to throw you off track.

Giving the presentation to someone who does not know the topic can be a great way to do the man in the moon test (see chapter 3). An outsider can't be expected to comprehend everything, but they can certainly help you to see the areas where you may not be as clear as you need to be. Also consider running the presentation past your contact, if you are presenting for a client of some kind. They may not want to sit through the entire presentation, but they will want to understand the approach you are taking and what you are covering.

Sometimes a client wants to do a dress rehearsal before the presentation. This often happens with clients such as advertising agencies. We meet the evening before and each person goes through their presentation. It is not always possible but when it is, it provides an additional layer of reassurance. (And also an additional opportunity to fail if you haven't done your own preparation ahead of time).

Practicing is also a great way to proof any audiovisual materials you are using. I was once doing a presentation for a national corporation. Fortunately, I was addressing a small group of people I had been working with so I had already established some credibility. I was working for a company at the time, and we had just hired someone whose job included developing presentations. He had followed my instructions carefully, it seemed. One of the PowerPoint slides I wanted to include was a map of the United States. Unfortunately, he took me a bit too seriously. That slide included a beautiful full color map with the bold headline: "Map of the U.S." I'd practiced my presentation, but only as I was traveling from one city to the next on a business trip. This practice had included only a cursory look at the slides—clearly a mistake of judgment on my part.

My audience guffawed when they saw the slide and thanked me for being so painstakingly clear. I came away from this experience embarrassed, but also aware of the importance of really practicing my presentation.

THE MYTH OF WINGING IT

I love spontaneity. I've sat in on presentations by people who seemed to be so comfortable that I could swear they were having a conversation with the audience, even if none of us were talking. They just seemed that relaxed and present.

Have you ever heard someone say about a hair style, "It takes me hours to achieve this casual windblown look?" The same goes for presentations. It takes a lot of hard work to make something appear "off-the-cuff."

I've sat on presentations where the speaker wanted to appear spontaneous but was instead demonstrating a complete lack of preparation. Since I am a presenter myself, I felt uncomfortable for them.

I have learned, in delivering presentations or facilitating groups in general, that my comfort level is built on a foundation of preparation. I can appear totally at ease, and totally engaged with my audience, if I am not mentally floundering around trying to figure out what to say next. The presentation has at some level to be second nature so that I can let my true nature come forth during the presentation. Preparation is the only way you can be spontaneous.

Chapter 6

Rehearsal

Practice is a crucial piece of the development process. After all, you're going to deliver your presentation, not read it. As you pull together the parts of your presentation, you get a feel for how the parts fit—like the scenes of a play, or, if you're more sports minded, the plays in a playbook. Some of them may fit together better in your head than in their planned positions in your presentation. Rehearsal helps you find these bumps and smooth them out before they cause your audience to stumble.

When you feel everything is in its proper place, you're ready to rehearse your presentation, start to finish. No more moving things around, no more changes, no more pausing to think about whether you want to say this or that. No faltering. No self-doubt. Rehearsal means running straight through your presentation, start to finish. Rehearsal is the final leg of the preparation triangle, the crucial last phase of getting your presentation ready for prime time.

Rehearsal is, itself, a process rather than a single event. I suggest three rehearsals, each of which focuses on one important dimension of your presentation:

- **Timing:** this rehearsal shows you how your presentation fits the allotted time.

- **Sound check:** this rehearsal lets you evaluate how you sound—are you too loud or not loud enough, monotone or lively, hesitant or confident?
- **Looks:** this rehearsal lets you assess your appearance, from what you're wearing to those mannerisms that may draw more attention than you realize or want.

Though I say three rehearsals, keep in mind you may need to repeat one or all of them several times until you get it down. So really, it's three sets of rehearsals. But believe me, it's well worth the effort. You'll be polished and confident when you deliver your presentation.

FIRST RUN: READ-THROUGH

No matter how great your presentation is, if it doesn't fit the time frame, it is not going to be a great presentation. You are either going to have to end it early or go into rush mode. Either way, you lose credibility and the opportunity to impart valuable knowledge, and your audience loses, too. Even though I practice the parts and pieces of my presentation during the development process, the first complete read-through is critical and sometimes sends me back to the drawing board because things don't fit into the whole in the way I practiced them as segments. Sometimes I feel silly rehearsing my jokes and thinking to myself, I hope I am pausing for a few chuckles at this point. And sometimes, in the context of the total presentation, the jokes that worked so well on paper don't fit anymore. Clearly, there are some small edits that occur after the first rehearsal.

You'll inevitably encounter rough spots and even places where you want to reorganize the material. Make a mental note to yourself when you hit these bumps but keep going.

The point here is to clock your presentation. Speak out loud, as though others were listening, but do this rehearsal alone. Use a clock or watch, rather than a timer, to time your presentation. The clock will be your timer during the actual presentation; rehearsing with it helps you develop a sense of time that integrates key points of your presentation with time markers. For example, your introduction may run 7 minutes, and at 20 minutes into your presentation you want to start your second objective. Keep your eye on the clock but don't watch it.

Many people, myself included, have a tendency to talk faster when nervous. So I concentrate on speaking slowly and clearly during my rehearsals, striving for the pacing I'll need for the actual presentation. What I find in my own presentations is that I tend to create more presentation than fits the time. Part of this is based on my desire to say as much as possible, and during the development process, one idea often leads to another. And part of it is the fear of not having enough, of running out of material. Dead time is definitely not a good thing! So what I often learn in this first run-through is that I have too much presentation for the time, but more about that later.

Time and Timing

This first rehearsal gives you a sense of both time and timing. Are your transitions smooth? Are you comfortable with your content and the logic of its organization? Do your audiovisual aids, including PowerPoint or other computer-generated materials, appropriately support and augment your content? Read through your entire presentation without stopping. If your presentation incorporates audience participation or writing on a flip chart or whiteboard, include these elements in your read-through. Ask the questions you anticipate from the audience, write on a flip chart (or piece of paper, for simulation). It's all too easy to structure a presentation to fit a time schedule and forget to allow for these "extras."

I'm kind of neurotic about time. I'm the guy that gets to the airport 2 hours before a domestic flight. I can't stand the stress of being late, of having to rush, of wondering whether I'm going to make it on time or not. And so I get to the airport well in advance of my flight. I don't have to be stressed out about the line at check-in or at security. I walk—not run—to the gate. Once there I can settle in and settle down. I might work on my laptop, read a book or magazine, or catch up on phone calls while I wait for my flight. When I'm running late, I become a different person. The stress really throws me off.

The same is true of presentations. Obviously I don't want to finish my presentation well in advance of the time allotted. My audience would feel cheated, and with good reason. I most likely would've left out some important details or rushed through my material so fast that the audience couldn't focus on half of it. Timing is not only about finishing on time. It is a way to protect yourself from the stress that can occur when you suddenly find your audience looking at their watches and you feel the urge to sprint toward the finish line.

During this first rehearsal, I get a feel for where certain milestones fit into the allotted time. Let's say I have one hour for my presentation. I may find that my upfront is taking 10 minutes, and the major details are taking 30 minutes, but I am still not allowing much time for the summary. I know I am going to want to take my time with the concluding comments. So I may establish a marker, say, 50 minutes, at the point where I am finally underway with the conclusions. If my rehearsal puts me at 1:05 by this point, then I know I'm five minutes over for a one-hour presentation. Because I don't want to rush my summary and conclusion, I know I need to go back to make a few cuts earlier in the presentation—maybe one or two of those jokes.

You may need to repeat this first rehearsal several times. But you want to nail down the details of timing before you move on to the other elements of delivering your presentation. Being off on timing or outside your time frame affects those other elements, and not usually in desirable ways.

The Timing of Questions

This first rehearsal is a good time to figure out how you're going to handle questions—will you take questions at any time during your presentation (not usually the best option though there are exceptions), at the end of key sections, or at the end of the entire presentation? I often do my first read-through without allowing for questions though keeping in mind that I'll need to accommodate them. How much time do I have left after I go through my content? With some kinds of presentations, such as reports (among the exceptions) that include lots of data and research findings, there are likely to be questions throughout. During this first rehearsal session—or perhaps the second or third run-through—I work to plan timing that allows for questions that interrupt the flow of my content.

It's sometimes difficult to figure out how much time to allow for questions. Your presentation rehearsal can help you identify places that naturally lend themselves to pauses and interruptions. Keep in mind that audience response and interaction will sometimes influence your presentation's time and timing in ways that you cannot entirely control. It's helpful to know what nuggets you can cut to accommodate the clock without dropping any key points.

SECOND RUN: HOW DO YOU SOUND?

The second run rehearsal lets you smooth out the edges of your presentation. Once you have the timing down and you are comfortable with the flow within the time frame, you can focus on your actual delivery. When I'm preparing for my second round of rehearsal, I ask myself:

- Who is my audience, and what do they expect from me?
- How do I find balance between the best way to address my audience and my own personal style?
- What is my tone and manner—my demeanor—going to be?

If you're thinking these questions seem familiar, you're right—they framed your presentation's development. During this second set of rehearsals, you have the opportunity to answer these questions in ways that guide how you'll integrate your personal delivery style into the presentation. If this is a training presentation, do you want to come across as the teacher? What does that mean? What is the best way to do this in terms of the material and the individuals in the audience?

I've done enough presentations now that I have a sense of how well I am adapting my style as I do the second-run rehearsal. I can hear it in my own voice, even feel it physically. But this was not the case when I first started presenting. I have a relatively soft voice. It sounds loud to me but not always to people around me. It took me awhile to figure out how to modulate my voice volume so that I know my audience can hear me. This means talking much more loudly, and articulating much more clearly, than was initially comfortable for me.

The volume and tonal quality of your voice is key to keeping your audience engaged. It also provides a framework for your audience for how to interpret and understand your content. Most people have fine voice characteristics for ordinary conversation. Nervousness and excitement, which are natural when giving presentations, can cause you to speak louder, faster, and at a higher pitch. You may stammer over words or pause at unnatural places in your sentences. But because you know what you're saying (or trying to say), you're not listening to what you're actually saying. Your audience, of course, has no idea what's in your head. So what comes out of your mouth is all they have to work with.

The Sound of Your Voice

Sure, you hear yourself talk. But the sound reaches your auditory nerves primarily through conduction via the bones in your face, giving it a different quality than it has when others hear your voice through conduction via airwaves. This is why, when you hear your recorded voice, you don't much sound like yourself—to you.

So this second run is also about making sure you are speaking with appropriate volume and articulation—your sound check. This rehearsal is to make sure you are loud enough but not too loud, and your words are clear enough for everyone in the audience to hear and understand. These are difficult qualities to measure on your own. It can be helpful to ask someone to sit in on this sound-check rehearsal—and is a must if you are a new presenter.

Your Test Audience

Ask a trusted coworker, friend, or your partner to sit and listen to you as a test audience. Sometimes, and especially when you're new to doing presentations, you may find it uncomfortable to "perform" in front of people you know. This, too, is part of the rehearsal process as well as your learning curve. It's important to feel comfortable and confident with your presentation no matter who's in your audience. Admittedly, this is sometimes easier said than done—but essential. Remember, your test audience is on your side.

If you have particular concerns, mention them so your test audience can be on the alert. Do you tend to say "uh" or "um?" These are empty space holders that your audience doesn't really need—they know you're thinking. Do certain words cause you to stumble or stammer? I know an executive, who makes a lot of presentations, who cannot say the word "aluminum." From his mouth, the word comes out "alunimum." Not such a common word in presentations but he practices the correct pronunciation.

Unlike the first rehearsal, which was a straight-through, this second rehearsal may proceed in fits and lurches. Be willing to stop, make adjustments in response to feedback from your test audience, and start over—sometimes again and again. Numerous elements of your presentation must come together, which is not always a smooth process. Far better to work out the glitches now, during rehearsal, than on-stage.

Play to a Virtual Audience

Don't have any live bodies to serve as your test audience? Don't fret! Set up an audiocassette tape recorder to create a virtual audience. Speak your presentation as though you had a real audience, and record yourself. When you replay the tape, listen to the quality and substance of your voice. Does it match your subject matter? Is your tone varied and interesting? Does the volume of your voice go up and down—appropriately for the content—or hang at a mind-numbing monotone? Simply listening to yourself can provide a wealth of information.

Voice Projection and Volume

Stand in front of your test audience (even if that's a tape recorder) when you do your sound-check rehearsal. Your posture affects your breathing and how you hold your head, which in turn affect your ability to project your voice. You can get the most from your voice when you stand upright with your shoulders back just a bit, which gives your chest the ability to expand for good, deep breaths. Hold your head upright, which extends your neck to give your vocal cords room to move. These details of posture let you speak forcefully without forcing the effort, allowing natural modulation to your voice even when you must be louder than normal conversation. You don't want to shout, which sacrifices tone for volume.

The Podium Factor

If you'll have a podium during your presentation, use one for this rehearsal. If you don't have a practice podium, use a small table or chair with a stack of books or boxes to roughly approximate the size and height of a podium. If you are short enough for the podium to reach no higher than your midchest, also use a small stool (short stack of books for your rehearsal) to lift your head fully above. This is an important detail, even though it might feel a bit silly, because there's a natural tendency to look down at your notes on the podium—and where your look focuses, your voice follows.

Will you have a microphone during your presentation? Then during your sound-check rehearsal you'll want to speak at a normal, conversational volume. The microphone will amplify your voice for you. It's good to become familiar with speaking into a microphone so you know how to position yourself. However, you're probably not doing your sound-check rehearsal in the same, or same-size, room that you'll be using for your presentation. But this is at least a start in terms of getting a feel for the ways in which you need to monitor your delivery.

When I first started doing presentations, I would occasionally have people in the audience cup an ear as a visual cue to get me to talk louder, or even ask me to speak up. I didn't love this, but I learned to speak in a louder tone. I may even ask the audience, at the beginning of the presentation, if they can hear me. Sometimes I'm still not able to judge how my voice is coming across, especially if it is being amplified—and I don't have control over the volume of the sound system.

Emotions and Passion

Emotions are part of your presentation. You may find that your passion for a topic comes forth in a positive way, and passion on the part of a speaker can really influence the audience's receptivity. But if your passion gets out of hand at times, this can be a problem. I don't just mean when you deliver a eulogy or are motivating an audience to adopt a new mind-set. You may be a trainer and really want your trainees to modify the approach to how they perform a specific task. Or you may be delivering a project update and be angry at the performance of one of the subcontractors in attendance at the presentation.

Do you have emotional landmines in your presentation? Where are they? How will you deal with them? This sound-check rehearsal can help you root out areas of your presentation in which your emotions may get the best of you.

I once did a presentation for caregivers, a topic I know a lot about from a professional perspective and I have been a caregiver myself. I came to the place in my presentation about how caregivers can't always help their loved one as much as they want. Whoops. A personal landmine. And I felt myself tearing up. I hadn't rehearsed the presentation in this regard and I had no idea this might happen.

I managed to pause and take a couple of quick breaths and then focus my mind on the next issue I wanted to talk about, and I managed to get through it. There is nothing wrong with showing some emotion, but it can make the audience uncomfortable.

If you ever took acting lessons, you might've been told the adage, "When you laugh or cry, the audience doesn't."

Anger is another emotion that can sneak out at the wrong time. If you are angry at that subcontractor, you may want to adopt a "reporter's attitude" at this point in your presentation to avoid letting your emotions—your anger—get the better of you. Part of this is psyching yourself up to get through certain parts of your presentation that might tap into your emotions.

THIRD RUN: HOW DO YOU LOOK?

Next up on the rehearsal agenda is an assessment of your appearance—how do you look when you take the stage? Speakers can emit personal tics and emotional cues without conscious awareness. You may not know what yours are until you have them reflected back in some way. Other people provide the most useful feedback because they see you in ways you do not see yourself. When you can't have a live test-audience, a mirror or a video camera are your next best options.

You might feel this third level of rehearsal is unnecessary. But if you're a new presenter, if you're using an approach that is unfamiliar to you, or if the presentation could make or brake (yes, brake—as in bring to a skidding halt) your career, this visual rehearsal is essential. For familiar or less significant presentations, you might be able to combine the sound-check and visual rehearsals into a single session.

Try not to feel hurt or angry with the feedback your test audience gives you about your looks and behaviors. Remember, this audience is on your side and is trying to help you be your best. That said, I freely acknowledge that it's not easy to hear unflattering comments about personal mannerisms and appearance.

Those Things That You Do

I often hold a red pen in my right hand when I give a presentation. And not just any red pen, it has to be a certain brand. My red pen is both security blanket and anxiety magnet: it makes me feel comfortable and it gives me a focal point for any tension and anxiety I might feel during my presentation. But after one presentation someone from the audience asked me why I was brutalizing my pen! Adding insult to injury, the presentation had been videotaped so I got to see exactly what the person meant. It took me a while to shift from cringing to laughing. Had that poor pen been a living creature, I'd have strangled it halfway through the presentation.

Now that I'm aware I can beat up my red pen to the point of distraction for the audience, I'm working on weaning myself from it. This is easiest when I have to turn pages or coordinate with a PowerPoint presentation, because these activities give my hands another focus.

Go Easy on the Button

When your presentation has audiovisual support, such as PowerPoint slides, your movements can distract from the points you're trying to make. Practice clicking buttons and moving the mouse until you can do so smoothly and unobtrusively. Your audience should not have a conscious awareness of these actions, even though of course they know you're doing them.

Because I know how hard it is to have other people point out personal habits, I'll share a couple of mine with you so you can feel better about yours. My nose itches when I am nervous. I may end up scratching my nose over and over during a challenging presentation. And, it seems, putting myself in front of an audience activates my throat-clearing reflex—no matter whether there's anything there to clear. This reflex, by the way, is common among speakers. Try having a glass of sparkling water at the ready to take small sips while you're doing your presentation. The carbonation will cut the tickle more effectively than plain water.

I've seen other presenters scrunch up their faces when trying to make a point. Women who constantly flick their hair back or run their hands through it. Men who constantly readjust their tie or check the zipper on their pants. Men and women who play with their jewelry—watches, rings, earrings. You may find your hand sneaking into your pockets, or you may have an unconscious desire to drum your fingers. Simply having someone tell you that you do any of these things draws enough of your attention to it that you stop.

Dress Rehearsal

You may even want to do this third round of rehearsals while wearing whatever outfit you are going to wear. This gives you a chance to make sure that your clothing fits—a lot can happen if you haven't worn an outfit in a year or so. It is something to consider especially at the start of a season when you suddenly must shift from one style to another.

I've experienced the fit crisis from both extremes. Once I chose a suit that I hadn't worn in over a year and, when I got dressed on the day of the presentation, found that it was too tight. Unfortunately, the presentation was in another city and I had packed only one suit. It was a very uncomfortable presentation because I felt and looked uncomfortable. Another time (in fact as a result of the too tight event), I found that my suit was too loose, especially in the pants. A dress rehearsal, or at least dressing up in advance of the presentation, would have prevented this.

If you can do a full-out rehearsal—the traditional dress rehearsal—in the actual location where the presentation is being held, so much the better, especially if includes some of the other people involved, such as the person introducing you. You can see how you work together, and make sure the introducer is not going to do or say anything that is going to throw you off, like give the wrong credentials or mispronounce your name.

With major presentations, this dry run is expected, though with smaller presentations it may not be possible. Even if you can't do a dry run, try to visit the location where you'll be doing the presentation while you have enough time to tweak things (in other words, further in advance than the morning before you do the presentation). You can quickly ascertain how you sound in the room, though keeping in mind that the sound will echo more in an empty room. If you can test the microphone in advance—and certainly before the actual presentation—this can also be helpful.

I often do visualization in advance of a presentation. This is like building in some quick dress rehearsals. I go to a quiet place where I can relax. I visualize the room where I'll be doing the presentation, or how I imagine it to be, and the audience. I visualize them as open and receptive to what I have to say. I see myself delivering the presentation with passion, authority, and confidence. I really stay focused on this image—how it looks and feels, and how it benefits my audience.

You may want to learn a relaxation technique or two and combine this with visualization. When you are actually about to present, draw upon your relaxation skills. I take measured, deep breaths to relax, while I sit up straight in a comfortable chair and then visualize my presentation. And then I use the same deep breathing to prepare myself to deliver my presentation.

GAPS AND GLITCHES

Regardless of your preparation and practice along the way, you are going to find some gaps in your presentation. Most of them should be obvious during your rehearsals—if not the first read-through, then most likely with the sound-check rehearsals. You'll catch some of these gaps yourself, and your test audience will identify others.

Glitches are the places in your presentation where potential problems may rear their heads. They are most likely to occur at points in your presentation where you must coordinate two or more events, such as lighting and visuals. Sometimes, for example, glitches result when you expect to have certain information and it is not available, or you discover too late that every third page in your handout is blank. (Though your pre-presentation checklist, chapter 7, should help minimize the likelihood of these problems.)

Two truths about glitches:

1. It is not possible to anticipate every potential glitch.
2. The more experienced with doing presentations you become, the broader your ability to cover and "wing it" when things do go wrong.

It's a good idea to practice, at least in your head, ways to continue your presentation without your planned visual aids or other support elements. What can you do if your presentation incorporates writing on flip charts to capture audience comments? What can you do if something goes wrong with your PowerPoint presentation? I talk more about glitches and problems in chapter 9, but your rehearsals are good opportunities to begin thinking about backup strategies. I also find that if I stay focused on my audience—meeting their needs for information, motivation, education—in my rehearsals as well as during the presentation, then I become less self-conscious and anxious.

After all, your presentation is a conversation. Admittedly, it is not exactly a two-way conversation—though, if you read body language, you can tell if your audience is involved. But I find that if I stay focused on meeting the needs of the audience, and on delivering something meaningful to them, then glitches along the way are not a big deal. I try to stay purpose-focused. If I am talking about a topic that I am especially comfortable with, such as stress management, I may even decide to take the presentation in a different direction, based on how the audience is reacting or something that I may have learned about them just before the presentation. I don't recommend this in a formal presentation, of course, but in any presentation I try to focus less on how I look and more on what my audience needs.

Chapter 7

Pre-Presentation Checklist

Now you're standing in the wings, it's nearly time to give your presentation. Your handouts are ready, your PowerPoint slides are dazzling, your notes are printed, and you have extra copies of everything. These next three chapters represent the final triangle of your presentation: checklist (this chapter), delivery (chapters 8 and 9), and the reviews (chapter 10).

The best presenters are so prepared, it appears they don't do much at all to get ready except walk to the podium. But rest assured, they have a not-so-secret stash of lists to check off and Post-It notes to remind them of what to do, when to do it, what to take, and who's responsible for doing what. You can never be too ready when it comes to the many details that will bring your presentation to life.

LISTS AND POST-ITS

In a perfect world I would focus on the big picture of my presentation while other people focused on the details. Details bore me, especially administrative details. They aren't any fun, they can clog up my brain, and they just add more anxiety for me—there's so much that can go wrong! So why not focus on what I do best and let all the details fall into place, or assume that other people who probably love details are going to handle all of them?

I also know that my reputation—and in the end, my presentation—depends on managing a lot of details. And when something does fall through, there is nothing worse than the attempts at goodwill or the out-and-out finger-pointing that follows. I've learned not to put all my trust in anyone else to handle the details, not even the people who are responsible for specific functions relevant to the presentation. I let those people do their jobs, but I check up on them—every last detail. Because, once again, my ability to give my presentation depends on it.

And I expect them to check up on me, to help me make sure I've done everything I need to do. In fact I ask them to. I tell everyone involved that we can really help each other out by checking up on each other. I ask them not to be offended when I call or e-mail and ask about something that I know they told me they would handle. I might even tell them that I am neurotic, I can't help it, and please humor me.

I also tell them that I have a lot on my mind and it really gives me some peace of mind to know that they will nag me. I might ask them to do it by e-mail so that I am not barraged with phone calls, and I do the same. I also ask that we please answer each other's e-mail within a few hours so that no one feels overlooked. Especially me. (I did say I'm kind of neurotic about these things, right?)

I've learned this approach the hard way. I've arrived to give a presentation only to find that no one had ordered the projector that would hook up to my notebook computer and allow me to display my PowerPoint slide show. I've also gotten to the presentation venue only to discover there was no VCR available. For other presentations, I've arrived and found that the copies of my handouts were not prepared—I'd sent the files or hardcopy, but no one had done anything with them. This is not a show stopper, but it can be frustrating and can add to the overall stress if it requires running around to get the copies made, collated, and stapled. It might be one of those days when the copy machine breaks down, or you're running late, or. . . . You never know what unexpected event can happen, which is why it's so essential to make sure everything is ready.

The Checklist Is Your Best Friend

Not so much a fan of lists? Time to change your tune—lists can save your presentation. Think of it: No flight ever leaves an airport without mechanics, ground crew, and flight crew checking off, item by item, numerous lists of details crucial to assuring a safe flight. You, as a passenger, wouldn't have it any other way. Your checklists as a presenter serve the same function. They safeguard you by catching details you've overlooked, and they help assure the best possible presentation for your audience.

In this chapter I've structured checklists to cover the basics that apply to most kinds of presentations. You're free to photocopy these checklists to use for your presentations. You may have other details that are specific to the presentations you do; write these on your copies so they become part of your routine. Make sure to include the deadlines and schedules of other people who have responsibilities, such as reserving the presentation venue, ordering refreshments, revising and proofing handouts, and coordinating the acquisition of any needed equipment and supplies. Some of the items on these checklists may not be relevant to you. As you do more presentations, you'll develop your own approach in terms of how you order and prioritize things.

PRODUCTION SCHEDULE

The production schedule identifies the dates by which certain elements of your presentation need to be completed. Most often, you'll start with the date of the presentation and work backward. Ideally, all of your production details should be completed and signed off far enough in advance of your presentation that you're not running around at the last minute, yet close enough that it's unlikely you'll need to update anything.

The Presentation

The core of your presentation is, of course, the presentation itself. You worked hard early in the process to research your topic, organize the information, create visuals, and document your sources. Most of the items on this checklist should've been completed long ago. Still, it's a good idea to go through these items to double-check. You'll want to be certain you've received the appropriate approvals and sign-offs, for example, before you step in front of your audience, even if you've already produced all the materials that support your presentation. Ideally you did this early in your process, but sometimes little details slip by—maybe your boss signed off but a committee member's signature is still missing from the approval document. Maybe someone was on vacation or out sick when the packet came around. Sometimes people forget, other times they have questions that somehow don't get answered.

Presentation Checklist

Element	Date Due	Date Completed
Create first draft		
Get reviewed		
Have proofread		
Create final draft		
Send for production		
Review final product		
Get final reviews		
Additional proofreading if changes are made		
Save on laptop		
Save backup copy on additional medium		
Send ahead to client		

The Handouts

Most presentations require handouts for the audience members. Yours may be as simple as an outline of the objectives and the time frame for the presentation. Or you may have charts, graphs, source documents, and even booklike bound materials. The more complex your handouts, the more lead time you need to allow for their preparation. It's a good idea to check with vendors such as printers even at the time you're considering what kinds of materials to use, so you can make sure you have enough prep time to produce what you want to use. I like to carry a clean, unstapled or unbound, set of handouts with me in case I need to do the old-fashioned and run (or send someone) to the copy machine or the corner copy store for rush reprints.

Handout Checklist

Element	Date Due	Date Completed
Create first draft		
Get reviewed		
Send for proofreading		
Create final draft		
Send for and required production		
Review final product		
Get additional reviews (if necessary)		
Additional proofreading if changes are made		
Save on laptop; backup copy to memory stick		
Create hardcopy to bring		
Send ahead to client (if necessary)		
Call client to confirm receipt		
Call client to make sure copies are made		

Audiovisual Elements

Who will produce your audiovisual materials, such as PowerPoint slides, video clips, and other media? Sometimes you choose this person, such as the video editor, and other times the person (or staff) is assigned to you. Perhaps this is an area of expertise for you, or your resources are limited, so you'll produce your own materials. In any case, there will be lead time involved. Make sure you have enough time to accommodate hiccups in the production process, such as overworked staff or being bumped by a higher priority project. I like to have a contingency plan in my thoughts so I can craft a work-around in a pinch. This might be shifting to a PowerPoint slide show I can put together myself, for example, or moving to a flip chart instead of printed poster boards.

Will the stakeholder have the equipment you need to use to display your audiovisual elements? How well does the room support your intended display? If you need to darken the room, for example, can you simply turn off the lights? Will there still be enough light for people to take notes or move around if they need to do that? A lot of the time you won't have much control over these variables but it's good to know about them.

Handout Checklist

Element	Date Due	Date Completed
Identify producer		
Create draft or audiovisual		
Obtain necessary reviews		
Create final version		
Obtain necessary reviews		
Get a copy on DVD or DC to carry with you		
If possible, save a copy on laptop		
If needed, send a copy ahead		
If sent ahead, confirm its receipt		
Make sure client has any needed AV equipment		
Call to make sure equipment is available		
Call to make sure equipment has been scheduled		

TASKS AND PEOPLE

Typically, other people have tasks related to your presentation. There's someone who takes care of reserving and arranging the room, someone who handles refreshments, someone who coordinates the production and delivery of your handouts and materials, and maybe even someone who takes care of your travel arrangements. Most of these people are already on other lists that you're using to keep track of your presentation's details. I find it helpful to have a master list of names, organizations, e-mail addresses, and phone numbers (including mobile numbers) for these people that I can quickly turn to when I have questions or concerns.

In the Cards

A card file is a handy way to keep track of people and their tasks, particularly if you do a lot of presentations that involve the same contacts. You can use a computer program to create the basic information, updating it for each presentation. Also print a hardcopy in a filing card size (and on filing card stock; versions for use with computer printers are available at office supply stores) so you have a paper record for your reference. Electronic methods, such as Blackberry and similar devices, are also great for quick access.

Your checklist may differ from what I use or with different kinds of presentations, so adapt my suggestions for your specific purposes. I try to keep things simple, so I set up my tasks and people checklist something like this:

Presentation Title: .... **Date:** ....

Contact Name
....

Contact Info
....

Task/Responsibility
....

Date Started
....

Date Done
....

....

I list each contact name for a particular presentation, and the person's responsibilities and due dates. This helps me to keep track of where these tasks are in the pipeline, and who I need to call to make sure it has happened.

CONFIRMATIONS

Check, double-check, and triple-check with the people you are working with to make sure they are in sync with your expectations, and that you are in sync with theirs. Keep in mind that people change functions and positions, and even leave the company. Depending on the lead time—the time between scheduling your presentation and your presentation's delivery—the people handling certain tasks and responsibilities may have moved to different departments and their replacements may not be up to speed on details such as your presentation. They may not yet realize that a ball is about to be dropped—they may not even realize there's a ball at all!

This may be the person who is supposed to have scheduled the room to be set up, or who would normally handle the handouts. You may be sending a file to someone who has left the company. And procedures often change—maybe the administrative assistant no longer makes copies, now there's a copy department to handle such tasks. The person handling your invoices, travel vouchers, and other financial details could have left the company and somehow your account didn't get assigned to anyone else. People tend to keep track of little details in their heads, which doesn't bode well when someone else has to step in or take over.

Confirming means not only calling or e-mailing and double-checking, it also means assuring that you and the other person are communicating—that you're on the same page. Repeat back what the person tells you and make sure you are both making the same assumptions. Even to the extent of making sure to identify the city and state, if you're traveling, or the date, month, and year as well as day of the week. These microdetails provide yet another level of checkback.

Someone may say, "Cleveland" and you assume Ohio—but the person meant Cleveland, Tennessee. Or someone may give you a date that doesn't match the day of week. I can't tell you the number of times little miscommunications cause major problems. I often follow up a phone or personal conversation with an e-mail that details what we have just talked about.

People also misinterpret or misunderstand each other for illogical reasons. You may discuss the need for a DVD player, yet even though the person you're talking to is saying, "DVD," he or she is thinking "VHS." You may want to tactfully make sure you are talking about the same medium or item, or you may arrive to find a VHS player and no way to use your DVD. Some words are difficult to understand or are commonly misunderstood in phone conversations, especially names. Always ask for spellings, to be sure. You don't want to arrive and ask for "Don" when you should be asking for "Dawn."

It seems repetitious but you need to follow up to make sure you should be sending something, and then follow up to make sure it got there. I try to not send items such as handouts until as close to the presentation as possible because sometimes I get last second brainstorms and I want the handouts to be as close to perfect as possible. As well, details such as the configuration or size of the audience may change. If you're sending your handouts as e-mail attachments, make sure your contact will have adequate time to make the copies. (And confirm this, in advance and again when you're confirming that the person has received the files.) Always, always, *always* make sure there is enough time for other people to produce the materials you need for your presentation. I can't stress this enough. No matter who drops the ball, the proverbial buck stops with *you* and you are the one who looks (and is) unprepared when items you need are not ready when you step to the front of the room.

LOGISTICS

It is critical to handle all of the little logistical details that can crash and burn your presentation. I try to plan in advance for this as much as possible. It saves last minute scrambling that can result in disasters. The details vary with each presentation, of course, but there are general key areas to consider.

Mailing and Shipping

For many presentations, you may carry everything you need with you. For others, you may need to send packages or files by e-mail to your contacts at the presentation venue. Notify recipients to expect your materials, and follow up to make sure they've received everything you sent. You're most likely to send ahead materials when you're traveling to do your presentation in another city, which means you may not have access to the original materials if anything goes wrong. So you want to confirm these details, and read back the responses to the person to double-check:

- When—date and time—are materials supposed to arrive?
- How are the handouts/materials being sent? (E-mail? FedEx? USPS? UPS?)
- To what address? (Mailing address? E-mail address?)
- To whom should the packages be addressed?
- Any special instructions on the label? (Caution: hotels can lose packages easily if items are not carefully labeled with your name and organization, and room number if known, or at least date of check-in.)
- If FedEx or UPS, whose account, mine or my contacts?
- Is someone going to be at the destination to pick it up? If so, who? If not, what are the arrangements?
- Who is going to verify receipt? Will someone contact me?
- Who can I call to make sure it arrived?
- What is the contingency plan if the materials don't arrive?

When you send materials via delivery service (FedEx, UPS, USPS, or other courier), obtain tracking numbers so you can determine the status of your packages. It doesn't cost much more to add a receipt verification. Packages get more careful treatment when someone has to sign for them.

Travel

Your only travel for your presentation may be on an elevator. Or you could be driving to another city or flying across the country. Make sure you know where you're going! This may sound like a no-brainer but it's easy to assume you know and then discover you don't have any idea where you're supposed to be. Obtain the exact address. Details about the building's appearance or location (for example, any nearby landmarks) are also helpful. You also need to know:

- Am I renting a car or taking a cab, or is someone picking me up?
- Do I have a map to give the cab driver or to use if I am driving?
- If the destination requires a flight, who is making the flight arrangements? The hotel arrangements?
- What are the travel guidelines I must follow if I am making the reservations?
- Is there a per diem for meals and related expenses?
- To whom will I submit my travel costs for reimbursement? Is there a form I will need to complete?
- If I am making my own hotel arrangements, what hotels does my contact suggest? How close are these hotels to the presentation venue?

Whatever travel is necessary, give yourself plenty of time to arrive well before your presentation. For distant destinations, I like to arrive the afternoon or evening before, so I can get a good night's rest and become somewhat adjusted to any time differences. For presentations that require travel to near destinations, I like to arrive a couple hours in advance of the presentation to find parking, locate the room where I'll be doing the presentation, and settle myself. I do much better when I don't have to rush—you will, too.

Arrival

You want to arrive at the presentation venue with enough time to make sure everything is set up as you want it or to finish setting up, depending on what all is involved. If there is a contact person who needs to facilitate this for you, it's important to make sure the person will be there when you want to arrive. Sometimes this involves balancing your preferences with your contact's expectations. Again, confirm these details in advance. You need to know:

- At what time may, or should, I arrive at the presentation venue?
- I may want to be one hour early, or more. Is that acceptable?
- Who should I ask for when I arrive?
- Who is meeting me when I arrive?
- If I want to arrive in casual clothes and then change, will I have time and a place to do this before I have to meet people?
- Will I be meeting with people first or go directly to the room where I am giving the presentation?
- Has time been arranged for me to briefly test my PowerPoint slides and any other audiovisual aids I am using? If not, do I need to arrive earlier than we had planned?

I like to be in the presentation room thirty minutes before my presentation. So I always confirm with my contact person that this can that be arranged. If this is a new venue, I may ask to be in the presentation room 45 minutes to an hour in advance, so I can familiarize myself with the location of the light switches, test the microphone and other equipment, and run through my presentation in my head in this setting. When there is nothing happening in the room before the presentation, this is not usually an issue. When the presentation is to be in a conference room, or in a setting that serves multiple purposes such as a cafeteria, scheduling becomes more critical and may limit advance access.

Some organizations require outsiders to be escorted for the duration of their time in the facility or building. Other organizations are more open and may allow you free access to the presentation room, coffee room, restrooms, and other areas. You may need to sign in at a central reception area or wear an identification badge while you're onsite. Will you be in an area that requires specific safety equipment, such as solid or flat-sole shoes (no high heels), steel-toe boots, a hard hat, or protective wear like a lab coat? Clarify these details with your contact person so you know what is expected of you.

Onsite Support

The presentation venue is your home away from home for the duration of your time there. You need to identify the resources available to you, and know what is required of you to access them. Information you need includes:

- Who will be my contact before and during the presentation? What are that person's e-mail address, telephone number, and cell phone number?
- What can I expect from my contact person in terms of availability or support? Where is that person located (building, floor, office) should I need him or her?
- Can I talk to this person and introduce myself before I arrive?
- Will this person run interference with the audiovisual people or will I do that?
- What about food? If I need to eat before my presentation, will food be available? Will there be someone to order it for me? Do I need to bring it myself?
- What about bottled water to have with me on the podium? (I bring my own water, just in case.)
- Are the handouts and any other materials going to be waiting for me? Where will they be?

- What if I need something unforeseen? Will there be someone available who I can call?

Many organizations have security procedures. You need to know before you arrive whether there are there restrictions on where you can go within the facility. You may need a security pass or to know a combination code for areas such as the restrooms and employee break rooms.

SUPPLIES

Some presentations require materials and supplies to be available for audience members. You're always better to have too many than too few; 10 to 20 percent is a good margin of safety in most settings. So if you have fifty people scheduled to attend a training presentation, you should have fifty-five (10 percent over) to sixty (20 percent over) books, sets of handouts, tools or instruments, or whatever items audience members will use.

At most presentation venues, I usually need:

- Flip chart.
- Markers for the flip chart.
- Bottled water.
- Paper for my notes, possibly pads to distribute to the audience.
- Writing implements for audience (I have my own pens).

If your presentation requires training manuals or other materials that the client or organization is supposed to provide, confirm that these are available and there are enough of them (this detail should be on your handout checklist.) Make sure you have the correct markers to use for your flip chart. Many general use markers will bleed through the paper, which at best means you need to use two pages for every one page you write on and at worst means you may leave your presentation notes on the walls of the room if you write on pages already taped up.

If you're using a whiteboard, use only whiteboard markers to write on it! Other markers may not erase. Though in a pinch you can use whiteboard markers to write on flip chart paper, you *never* want to use flip chart markers (or overhead markers or highlighters) on a whiteboard. No matter what your writing surface, try to use odorless markers. Some markers are scented, such as fruity. Others just smell bad.

Personalize It!

Are you providing writing implements such as pens, pencils, or even highlighters, for audience members? This is a good opportunity for a little shameless self-promotion for you or your organization. It doesn't cost much to order personalized items, from pens to writing tablets. Your company may already have items you can use, or you may choose to order your own.

YOUR PRESENTER'S TOOL BAG

I try to anticipate what I might need at the presentation venue and to be ready for whatever might go wrong. So I carry these items with me:

- Hardcopy list with all of my contact information (names, phone numbers, and cell phone numbers).

- Highlighter or a red pen to use on my notes.
- Extra markers for the flip chart (or whiteboard if I'm using one).
- Breath mints/strips (your mouth can really get dry quickly).
- Extra bottle of water and some snack foods.
- Flash drive in case a file has to be moved from my laptop to someone else's.
- Laptop and power cord (don't depend on the battery, even if you have a replacement one).
- Clean set of handouts (in case I need to make more copies).
- Presentation on alternate media (such as printouts of PowerPoint slides).
- Any needed backup notes or documents that I may need to rely on during the presentation if a question arises.

As you become more experienced in giving presentations, you may find that your presenter's tool bag includes items such as Post-It notepads, pens or pencils and writing paper you can pass out to audience members who arrive without them, a whiteboard eraser, and a roll of masking tape to hang completed flipchart pages on the walls. Paperclips, pushpins, chalk (yes, every now and then you encounter a real blackboard!), a few sheets of peel-and-stick labels, and 3x5 or 4x6 cards (great for spontaneous exercises or activities, or to create name placards) are also handy to have with you.

CONTINGENCY PLANNING

Contingency planning is about covering the what-ifs. In some ways, I am doing contingency planning all the way through the process—by asking people if they are doing their parts, making sure we are confirming, assuring that I have backup, and so forth. It's a good strategy to rehearse your presentation without your planned audiovisual or PowerPoint materials, to cover the potential for technical or equipment glitches that would require you to do this at the actual presentation. I basically assume that Murphy's Law can hit at any moment, and then I prepare for as many of those moments as possible. You cannot prepare for everything, of course. But the more bases you cover (as previous chapters discuss), the better prepared you are for common—and not so common—challenges.

Chapter 8

Show Time!

After all the preparations, the time is finally here to wow the audience with your presentation. From setting up to closing down, you're on—it's time to bring your presentation to life. If you've rehearsed your presentation and really tweaked it into a solid, smooth-flowing production, you might think delivering the actual presentation is a done deal. In some ways, it is. If you have a firm foundation in your presentation, you should be in great shape at this point. But the real deal takes on a different dimension and a life of its own. Your audience has a vested interest in what you're about to say or do (and may have even paid for the privilege of being there). And your audience becomes part of your presentation—a factor you can prepare for but can't fully rehearse.

SETTING UP

Most of my presentations take place in small conference rooms, training rooms, or company lunchrooms. My audience may be sitting in chairs and desks, classroom style, or in a circle, or around a table. Major presentations may take place in an auditorium, but this is not common for me. No matter the situation, however, I find out exactly how the room is going to be set up and make sure that any special needs are going to be met.

Sometimes I have the luxury of doing a genuine dress rehearsal, a full run through my presentation with all its bells and whistles, maybe the night before or the day of, in the actual room where the presentation is going to happen. Then I can be really sure that the setup is perfect because I'm able to test it. But usually, someone else handles the setup arrangements—from room selection to seating for the audience—and you don't quite know what to expect until you walk into the room.

Here are some details you'll want to address before, so to speak, the curtain goes up:

- Is the microphone in place and either on or already sound-checked for volume?
- Is there an outlet or an extension cord to plug in your laptop?
- Does your laptop work as you need it to? (Useful but quirky devices, those laptop computers.)
- Is any other audiovisual equipment in place, plugged in, and tested?
- Do you have water available?
- Are handouts and other audience materials ready?
- Do the seating arrangements make sense for the composition of your audience and for the style of your presentation?

If you are speaking to a large group, a microphone is essential. I have a relatively soft voice, and I'm tall. That can present two problems for me with the microphone. It has to be turned up loud enough to catch my voice. And it has to be high enough for me to talk into without hunching over. Shorter people have other concerns. The microphone may be too high or too far away or may block the audience's view of your face.

Given my soft voice, after I greet the audience, I ask them if they can hear me. It takes only a few seconds, I can make any necessary adjustments, and then we move on. This is an important part of the setup and one that you may need to handle when you actually get going.

If my presentation takes the round-the-table format in a conference room (which sometimes does double duty as the cafeteria), I determine where I'm most comfortable sitting and then I place my water and notes at that spot. Of everyone at the table, I am the one who most needs to be in a comfort zone, the one who can have the best eye contact with everyone else in the room, and the one who must leverage my voice.

I might ask that some adjustments be made—the temperature, the position of the table. If it is a classroom, I might ask that the podium be moved, or that I be provided with a table. Or I might want the chairs rearranged to facilitate interaction. It is important to give yourself permission to be high maintenance. You are not only the presenter but most likely the closest thing to an expert on presentations. Only you know what is optimal for your presentation and your presentation style.

I can be a bit sarcastic about the conditions of a venue, especially if I'm nervous or frustrated. I was giving a presentation at a conference. The five presenters sat at a head table and then took turns presenting at a podium. The conference was at a mediocre Manhattan hotel. The sound system wasn't great. I got up to the podium and the microphone was way too short unless I wanted to stoop to try and talk into it. I played around trying to adjust it and it was clearly an old piece of equipment. I looked around for someone to help.

Finally, in frustration, I said, "either someone has to raise this so that I can stand up straight or lower it and I will just do the presentation on my knees."

That got a few laughs, mostly from my friends when I told them about it afterward, but came out a bit too angry, I'm afraid, and it didn't result in any changes during the presentation. I felt like if I had taken note of this ahead of time, and asked someone in charge how to fix it, I would have been a lot better off.

AND NOW, OUR MAIN FEATURE

Usually there is someone to introduce you to the group. If you're making a presentation to your peers or to upper management, this person is likely your supervisor or manager. If you're making a presentation to an audience of strangers, the person who introduces you is usually the person who arranged for you to do the presentation.

Walk purposefully and confidently to the front of the room, or step forward if you're already standing in front of your audience. Thank your introducer, then turn your attention to your audience. If you will be speaking from a podium during your presentation, step to the side or in front of it during your opening remarks. This makes you seem more approachable—there are no barriers between you and your audience.

Take a slow, deep breath (discreetly) before you begin to speak to the group. It's fine to take a moment to gather yourself. The members of your audience are probably still shifting and arranging themselves, so a brief pause helps them to settle down. Try to stand comfortably yet professionally. If you're sitting with the group around a table, lean forward slightly so everyone can see your face.

GREETING YOUR AUDIENCE

I always greet my audience with a good morning or good afternoon. I thank them for giving me the opportunity to talk to them. Starting out with some humility is a good way to begin to win over your audience. Then I ask if everyone can hear me. I don't always know how I am projecting. Someone may be hard of hearing or be sitting next to the air conditioner. Large group, small group, I do the same sound check. This is practical because it assures that I am being understood. It also lets the audience know that I value them, and the opportunity, so much that I want to make sure they can hear every word.

I also make sure to provide as much eye contact as possible when I greet the audience. I look around the table, or around the room, and take a pause while I try to acknowledge as many people as possible. It's not necessary that I know these people, although when I do I might acknowledge them more personally. This draws the audience in and makes a connection with me. And it gives me a chance to also feel a connection with them. It is a chance to gauge their mood—do they smile, look away, look distracted, look back blankly?

Cover Your Nervous Memory

Take a moment to WRITE the name of the company you are speaking at and the names of any key people you will need to mention at some point in the presentation. Chances are, you may forget or confuse their names if you get nervous. I worked for a company that had an annual conference for customers. One year, we were in Boston. We hired someone who wrote a local Boston newspaper column to give a light presentation about Boston at lunch. He opened with some jokes about Boston accents, the traffic, etc. Soon after that, he said how happy he was to be talking to the employees of the XYZ company. Only, guess what: we were the ABC company and XYZ company was our key competitor.

If they don't seem receptive, this doesn't mean the presentation is going to go badly. There may be a lot of people who are having a hard day, or maybe they are feeling a lot of pressure. They might be unsure what to expect, or still thinking about what they were doing before they came to the presentation. Maybe their corporate culture just isn't all that friendly. I have learned to look at this as an opportunity to bond with them, even if they aren't greeting me with open arms. And if they are receptive and smile back, then so much the better.

In a small group, such as when sitting around a table or in a classroom, I might make a comment about how they respond. I might joke about how skeptical they seem, or depending on the subject and the level of the people, I might ask if they are in a bad mood. But that depends on the group and is a matter of judgment.

I always try to mention something off-topic at first. If I am not from their area, I might tell them how much I enjoy being there, or something funny that happened to me. Or some local sight I saw, or food that I enjoyed (or didn't!). Often, I say something that one-downs me, maybe something funny about something absentminded I did, or how I misunderstood something. I don't go overboard, or on and on, but something just enough self-deprecating to get a few chuckles.

When you are nervous, this kind of interaction may be difficult. Remember to breathe and relax. These are only people—and you know how to engage with people, right? Keep your level of banter in a zone that is comfortable for you. Though humor is a great icebreaker, keep the jokes—especially those that poke fun at anything or anyone other than you—in check.

ESTABLISHING EXPECTATIONS

Chances are everyone in the audience knows why you are there—whether it is a group of eight or a room of 800. They know who you are, why you are speaking, what you are speaking about, and what they expect to learn from you. Or at least, they think they do. But if you did a brief experiment and asked each person to write down their answers to these questions, you would most likely get as many different answers as people in the room.

So you need to remind them. This can be as simple as opening with, "I'm here today to talk to you about . . . to report . . . to explain. . . . " Then follow with a brief summary of your topic and your key objectives. Because in reality, not everyone has come to the presentation with the same understanding of what to expect. They may have missed the memo but talked to someone else, made a good guess, or been tapped for attendance at the last minute. They may have heard but forgotten. Or what they heard got twisted up with their expectations or what they hoped you would be presenting.

I might also briefly mention some limitations, such as:

- Due to time or other constraints, we will briefly review one topic but spend more time on another.
- A project update may include only what has happened within the most recent phase.
- I am training on a certain procedure but not a range of procedures.
- Because of my background, I am being brought in to talk about one specific topic but won't be able to address other questions or issues.

I make sure the audience knows where I am going. This helps them to listen because they now don't have to be thinking, *I wonder if he is going to talk about. . . .* And it helps me because if the audience has expectations I am not going to meet, then they are going to leave unhappy. If our expectations don't meet, I can't win. This shows up in their questions—they may toss out questions that have no relationship to why I am there. And because they expected one thing and I delivered something else, they may give me a bad evaluation.

INTRODUCING YOUR PRESENTATION

After I set expectations, I might go through a list of topics. This lets the audience know exactly what I am going to cover, orients them to my format, and lets them know how they should expect the presentation to flow. This sets up a template in their mind that they can use to begin to mentally hang the information on.

I often introduce the presentation with a story. Audiences love stories and examples, which really bring your concepts and material to life. I can watch them visibly perk up, whether a small group or a large group, once I start to tell a story. I might tell them something from my own experience, or I might pick an example that relates to the topic, or maybe something I read in the newspaper. This pulls them in. It also establishes my experience and involvement and gives me credibility. And it automatically makes the topic relevant to them.

I can't emphasize enough the importance of introducing the presentation in a way that is meaningful to your audience. In spite of the fancy credentials you may have, and may have been indicated to the audience in advance, you still have to establish your credibility. This is especially critical if you are a designated presenter or when doing a presentation to your peers who have their own ideas about who you are that might be more narrowly focused than gives you credit for knowing your stuff.

And Assisting Me Today Will Be . . .

When I introduce my presentation, I may also let the audience know what props I will be using. I might let them know that I will be taking them through a PowerPoint presentation while I talk, for example. They may have the hardcopy of the presentation. I let them know about any video clips I am using, why I am using them, and where they came from. I might also make a joke about how my father sent me to college because I am so mechanically inept. Then if there is a glitch along the way, we can quickly chuckle about it and move on.

If you use an example from your own experience, then you show the audience that you know what you are talking about, or that you have really thought about the topic, or their organization, beyond just throwing some facts together (if it were only this easy, you say, after all that practicing and rehearsing). There are many sources for relevant connections.

By the time you are standing in front of your audience, you should already know what stories you want to tell—this is part of developing your presentation (chapter 4). You may have a handful of stories from which you choose, depending on the actual audience configuration or response at your opening remarks. Because I do a lot of presentations to diverse groups, I now have quite a collection to draw from, and I'm comfortable with somewhat winging it to weave in events of the day or other such details specific to the audience.

If I am talking to counselors, I might use an example from my own practice. If I am talking to researchers, I might talk about an example from the research—something that occurred during the work. Or I might tell people from a company that I saw one of their products in use. That somehow relates to the topic, but on a much broader level. This indicates that I think this is important, and that what I am talking about relates to the real world. I may open with something that I read in the newspaper, or mention a commercial I saw that in some way shows a connection between me/my topic and the audience. A bonus is that this compliments the audience in a way that endears you to them.

I might talk about a conversation I had with someone in the audience's organization (only do this if you've obtained permission from the person whose conversation you're about to divulge) that compliments that person and establishes that I've been extensively involved. With medical professionals, I might talk about a friend or relative who suffers from the condition they treat.

I might also talk about how the topic has affected me personally, how it has challenged me, or taught me something I didn't know, or somehow changed my life. I work in patient decision making for a large cancer center. I often tell them how that experience changes my life in some way, and it certainly does.

I may introduce myself in terms of my background, if that hasn't been done for me. I try to tell the audience aspects of myself and my expertise that I think will be relevant to them specifically and uniquely, that is of interest to them and not just a litany of my resume. Nobody likes someone who just appears to be bragging—it gains you no respect.

DELIVERING YOUR PRESENTATION

I feel that every presentation I do, I deliver in a different way even when it's the same content and format. This is a function of who is in the audience, the topic, the objectives, and other such details. The size of the audience also has a lot to do with a presentation's delivery—a small group or a large group, the organization of the room—as well as the presentation's length.

But there are some elements of presenting that are essential to keep in mind for any presentation.

These include:

- Make eye contact.
- Breathe.
- Slow down.
- Pause.

Your presentation notes (chapter 4) should include brief but explicit directions for where you need to integrate audiovisual materials, including PowerPoint slides. I'm diligent about this because I assume there is the possibility my mind may go blank when I am in the middle of my presentation. I reassure myself by adding notes that will allow me to get help whenever I need it.

Eye Contact

Eye contact is important. The audience, small or large, needs to feel like you are engaged with them as individuals. While you may avoid eye contact out of genuine nervousness, they may interpret it as insincerity or as evidence that you are uncomfortable or unfamiliar with your material. But if you are too nervous, you may find yourself making too much eye contact with one person, or looking only at the people who smile at you. At some point, the other audience members notice and may feel overlooked or wonder if you have a hidden agenda.

I try to pick a pivot point in the audience, somewhere in the center. This happens if I am sitting at a table or addressing a large group. This pivot point might be one person or it might be the center of the group. I remind myself not to use this as my focus but to use it like a landing strip. I start there and then rotate my head from right to left. I also remind myself not to forget people who are sitting at my immediate right or left.

Flip Charts

Are you using a flip chart during your presentation? Remember that markers often bleed through the paper. Once you tear off a page and tape it to the wall, consider it finished. If you add to it after it's hanging, you could truly end up with writing on the wall! It's better to use a fresh page for additional thoughts, and then tape it next to the first one.

Obviously I can't move my head back and forth continuously—this would be a little jarring for the audience not to mention dizzying for me—but I do try to make eye contact with each person at the table or in the small group periodically, and with each section of the room from time to time. This increases the connection with the audience and makes me both look and feel more self-confident. And while you may really appreciate those audience members who nod their heads and smile in a spirit of active listening, don't get lured into making them your only focus because you may leave behind the rest of the group.

Breathe

Breath—how I use my breathing—is key for relaxation and control of your body, thoughts, and emotions. I get nervous sometimes, and I may talk too fast and not take enough time to breathe. My words can begin to run into each other. This also happens when I am excited. Breath control means to breathe, literally, but it also means to relax. I may combine a deep breath with a pause, which helps both me and my audience to take it down a notch.

Slow Down

"Slow down" works the same way as "breathe," but it is telling me to pace myself, not to rush through the presentation.

And if I have rehearsed it for time (chapter 6), I remind myself that I know I have plenty of time so I can pace myself without running out of time or finishing too early. Complicating the issue of timing for me is the reality that I'm not very mechanically inclined and even with a lot of practice there are times when I may make mistakes as I move forward in the PowerPoint presentation or back and forth between my presentation and the video clips or something in between. I have been known to move back instead of forward in my presentation.

Pause

Taking a pause here and there provides a moment for your audience to let your words sink in. A pause also signifies that you have just said something especially important and you want them to think about it before you move on. Or a pause can signify that you are moving to the next topic or thought, so in that way it is transitional.

My presentations often include the drinking of water, at least for me. I get dry mouth easily, whether or not I am nervous. When I talk a lot, I get a dry and scratchy throat. I may try to time the slug of water so that it appears after a point I am trying to make, so that I combine it with a pause.

AUDIENCE PARTICIPATION

When you are addressing a small group, such as ten or so people sitting at a table, it is a good idea to try to make your presentation as interactive as possible. When you are this up close and personal, people expect to interact with you. I often make presentations for employee assistance programs, topics like stress management, and in a small group, the audience gets much more involved if there is extensive interaction. People are more comfortable talking in a small group.

I am careful about calling on people. If the members are not volunteering to speak, but one person is giving me a lot of eye contact and seems involved, I might ask the person if she or he wants to add anything. I try not to put people on the spot with direct questions. If you are open and comfortable and friendly, people will interact with you.

With experience, I have learned to turn a presentation into an ongoing conversation, in which I provide information and techniques, but in concert with the audience. I have learned to follow up on what they say, turn it into larger meaning, and then weave that back into the group. That takes a lot of practice. When you are starting out, giving your talk, and then pausing to see if anyone has comments, will provide enough interactivity.

With a somewhat larger group—more than twenty people—you can also be somewhat interactive, just in a more controlled manner. You might offer the audience the opportunity to question or comment, but be careful to stay on topic.

Reinforce Interactions

It is important to reinforce every person who talks. Comments such as "that's interesting" or even a simple "thank you" acknowledge the speaker and let the audience know you really do want to hear from them. But if you leave a pause after someone talks but don't comment, or cut someone off, you leave them feeling disrespected.

In a larger audience, you may want to carefully limit participation to stay on track and on time. It's also a challenge, at times, when a few people dominate interaction. It's easier for this dynamic to develop in a large group so you need to stay on top of it. I do think that adults have attention spans that are no better, or even worse, than those of children. So they can't be lectured at for too long. They get bored and tired even if you think you are interesting. So I try to build in some audience participation (ideally, you've done this during your presentation preparations). Even in a large audience, I might give them a five-minute assignment. Something like, share an experience you have had that illustrates this principle. Or, break into small groups and talk about how you would implement this strategy. And I never talk more than an hour without providing a break.

FIELDING QUESTIONS

Your rehearsal sessions (chapter 6) are your first opportunity to experiment with the matter of audience questions. To some extent, the reason for your presentation and the topic blend to shape audience interaction. If you are presenting the findings of a report, you probably want your audience to listen through all of what you have to say before asking questions because your later content is likely to answer questions that arise in the early part of your presentation. In other types of presentations, it may be smoother and more productive for the audience to ask questions throughout the presentation (such as during training presentations).

Establish the Ground Rules

When I set expectations regarding the scope of the presentation in my introduction, I often also indicate how I want to handle questions. I might say, "Feel free to interrupt me with questions." When I do that, I have most likely built a lot of extra time into my presentation, or I have an open-ended time slot. But I might also say, "If you ask about something that I am going to cover later, I may ask you to please be patient because I will get to it." Or I might say, "Please hold your questions until the end. But if I need to repeat or elaborate on something, please let me know."

Stand by whatever rules you set. You can't indicate that questions need to wait until the end and then let someone jump in and ask a lot of questions. You need to gently and graciously remind that person that you want to keep the flow going and respect the audience members' time, so you appreciate everyone holding their questions until the end. The one exception, bowing to corporate politics, is when the questioner is the "alpha dog" in the group—the senior vice president or some such executive. In such a circumstance it's usually prudent to indulge the question.

In training presentations, I pause periodically to ask for questions. This keeps the audience involved and makes sure that I don't go too far without everyone being on the same page. Yet a research update may require that questions be saved until the end because you don't want people questioning the results until they've seen all of the results. Such questioning can throw you off-track as well as confuse the presentation because you end up giving information out of sequence or out of context.

You might also pause and specify the kinds of questions you are open to answering. You might say, "Any questions about why we decided to do it this way?" Or, "Anyone unsure of what I mean by that?" This signals that questions can be asked, but only within certain parameters.

Some presentations are just going to have a lot of ongoing questions because it's the nature of the group. If it is a group that is in the midst of strategy, then they can't hold their questions until the end. They need to interrupt, question, and maybe talk among themselves. To attempt to deny this process establishes you as rigid and the group dynamic will overrule you. But I might gently remind a group like this that what they are questioning is going to be discussed further down the road, or that we are getting short on time, unless they want me to go overtime. This establishes that you understand their interests and needs but are also being mindful of the predetermined parameters for the presentation.

Peripheral Questions and Submerged Issues

If you are going to be in a situation where you will do a lot of interaction with the audience, whether large or small, keep in mind that you are going to get a lot of questions that are peripheral to the presentation—in other words, topics that don't relate directly to your presentation but are of interest to the audience. Sometimes this interest is within the context of your subject, but your presentation has a more narrow focus. In these situations, I bring a lot of notes along that I carefully organize so that I can reference them quickly.

Other times the interest arises from icebergs that you may or may not know about before you begin your presentation. These submerged issues may have to do with company policies and procedures, corporate culture, the workplace environment, or any number of other circumstances that affect the ways in which your audience perceives what they're expected to do with the information you're providing.

Sometimes you cannot address such questions—it might be beyond the scope of your presentation or your expertise, it could be restricted information, or it could be so much of a digression that it entirely derails your presentation. While there are times when you need to be flexible enough to go with the flow even when it changes your course, most often you want to stick to your designed presentation.

CONCLUDING YOUR PRESENTATION

I always go back to the rule of thumb: Tell them what you are going to tell them, tell them, and tell them what you told them.

As part of my formal presentation, I've already included a brief summary of key points that I review at the end. I make sure I allow adequate time to go through these points and give each one of them its appropriate emphasis. I make a lot of eye contact with audience members and carefully articulate each point. This may be that part of your presentation—other than whatever levity you provide at the beginning—that your audience remembers most.

If you rush through the summary you risk leaving the audience confused, appearing less than organized yourself, and potentially telegraphing that you tossed out a bunch of stuff and hope that they find a way to make sense of it later on. This should all be built into your presentation and carefully rehearsed. It is key for a solid conclusion.

I come full circle with my conclusion to end with a round of thank-yous, just as I started the presentation. If I had an internal contact—an HR person, a research manager, a marketing manager—I give that person a special thank-you for his or her collaboration and assistance. This not only gives key people some recognition but also implies to the audience that I am an extension of their team.

If there was a support person or two who helped me, I also mention them by name (though if you are going to this, make sure you use the correct name and pronounce it correctly). This person most likely deserves recognition more than anyone. And I again thank the audience for being so welcoming, such good listeners, so interactive, for asking such interesting questions—whatever specifics are appropriate. Finally, I open it up for any additional questions, if time permits. Or I say, "I have time for maybe two questions" to set expectations. Depending on the format, I may also offer to stay around for a while afterward if someone wants to talk to me individually.

Then it's time to pack your stuff. Make sure you get all your power cords, extension cords, extra handouts, markers, pens and pencils, and any other supplies or materials that you brought with you. It's also good to tidy up a bit—throw away obvious trash, put tables and chairs back if you moved them, erase the whiteboard, and so on. The real cleaning is not your responsibility, of course, but making the effort to restore your environment to a presentable state is a gracious gesture.

Chapter 9

Handling Challenges

Presentations are a fine example of the 20/80 rule: 80 percent of the time, the presentation goes off without a hitch, much to the delight of the audience and the presenter. The other 20 percent of the time, however, challenges arise. You're way ahead of the game when you can meet that 20 percent with humor, grace, and confidence.

KEEP YOUR SENSE OF HUMOR

Humor helps you maintain internal balance so you can project an outward image of unflappability. After all, you're the expert and experts are supposed to be innovative and collected. Panic? Not you! You smile and laugh even when things get frustrating or tense.

It's not always natural or easy to stay upbeat and positive in times of challenge, but it's definitely more effective and pleasant—for you and for your audience—than becoming irritable and belligerent. I've become quite good at finding the humor in awkward situations and at making jokes at my own expense. I've come to recognize that everyone knows what it's like to have things fall apart, and that mishaps and misadventures happen to everyone.

I was giving a very important presentation on some international research that I conducted for a company that makes notebook computers. A PowerPoint slide show with embedded video clips was the basis of my presentation, displayed on a notebook computer. (No, it was not the company's brand of notebook computer.) The presentation was also being webcast to employees in a dozen other locations.

Halfway through the presentation, my notebook froze. Just stopped, dead in its tracks, with no warning. Fortunately a colleague was in the audience who had the PowerPoint slideshow on her notebook computer. She fired it up, paged forward to the correct place in the presentation, and we switched computers. I was lucky beyond lucky.

By this time, the audience knew what was going on. So I said, "I just learned a lesson here. If I don't use one of your products, then I better have a backup. And it better be one of your products."

Someone in the audience yelled, "Yeah, [brand name] to the rescue!" I laughed and blushed, and then the program went on.

When something doesn't go quite right when you are doing a presentation, you need to be ready to break the tension. It's awkward for you, certainly, but also awkward for your audience. They're waiting to see how you're going to respond before they react. When you have a sense of humor about it, you relieve your own internal tension, and that is especially important. If you are tense inside, you are going to freeze up, like that notebook computer, or blow up, or get completely off track. A smile or a laugh releases all of the pent-up emotion, and you clear your head. I don't mean make a big joke out of something that is important to your audience, but handle it with a smile.

And competent people have a sense of humor about what is happening around them. They can have this sense of humor because they are the experts and they have the confidence to know that they can handle anything that comes their way. And as long as the audience believes this about you, it's probably true.

LATE ARRIVALS AND EARLY DEPARTURES

I get annoyed when people come in late or leave early—whether it is a large group, a small group, or a class that I am teaching. It throws me off stride. The disruption interrupts my rhythm, and sometimes I spend the rest of the presentation struggling to regain my momentum and equilibrium.

I'm the kind of person who's generally running *early* to meetings. I don't like to arrive late. I feel like a slacker when that happens, and it feels disrespectful to the other people attending, including the presenter. When the meeting involves business clients or counseling clients, being late is out of the question. But lateness happens. Things happen that make people late, and they have no control over them. This is what I remind myself when I am the presenter and I am feeling that flush of annoyance when someone comes in late.

There are a number of ways to handle latecomers; I don't use any one of them as a standard approach. It really depends on the size of the group and the make-up of the audience and the topic. When the group is small, I usually briefly acknowledge the latecomer, politely but not necessarily warmly. Maybe the person couldn't help it; I like to give people the benefit of the doubt. Also, if I introduced myself to the group in my opening remarks, and we exchanged names, then I also introduce myself to this person. If I am just getting into the presentation, I might quickly recap to bring the person up to speed. If am further in, I just identify where I am in the conversation.

The MIP Exception

If the latecomer is a most important person (an MIP, you might remember from chapter 3)—for example, the head of the project or an executive—I ask if he or she wants me to briefly review what I have talked about so far. This is a sign of respect and probably necessary anyway.

With a large group, I try not to miss a beat when a latecomer walks in. Now, if there are a series of latecomers, this isn't always easy. And if a handful of latecomers come in at once, I might pause for a moment and let them get seated. I won't keep doing that, but I might do it the first time it happens. Occasionally, I make a joke, for example, say something like "you're late" but with a smile. It is an opportunity to lighten the atmosphere before I proceed.

The same goes for people who leave early. I once did a presentation through a company's employee assistance program. I walked into a room of maybe ten people. As I walked in, four of them got up and left, as if on cue. Now, how do you think I felt? I smiled as they were leaving and said something like, "Was it something I said? Is it my tie?" One of them was polite enough to turn around and say that they had just been paged to take care of an emergency in the computer room. I was glad that I'd made a comment because, I have to say, the experience temporarily took the wind out of my sails. Knowing the exodus had nothing to do with me personally made it possible for me to regain my composure.

In a large group, chances are that people will start trickling out before the presentation ends, especially if the meeting is not mandatory. At conferences, this is really common. The truth of the matter is that adults have short attention spans. And they have a low tolerance for information that is not relevant to what they are specifically interested in. You can't be totally relevant to everyone all the time. Some people will listen for the information they came to hear and just get up and leave after that.

It's okay. It's not you.

INTERRUPTIONS

I try to minimize interruptions. They disrupt my flow and they break the audience's concentration. I've had to learn to be more tolerant. Sometimes I do presentations in rooms that have other uses, such as the employee lunchroom. Even when we reserve the room, employees can still come in to get coffee or grab their lunches out of the refrigerator. I don't like this but it's their routine and not intended to disrupt my presentation or bruise my ego. Sometimes someone will walk in and ask to speak to a person in the audience. I just pause and wait for that person to acknowledge the request, and then I proceed. Again, I know this is not directed at me.

Other external, or environmental, interruptions may come in the form of sirens, planes landing and taking off, when your venue is near a major airport, or even equipment failures such as the microphone cutting out or a power outage. These events are beyond your control and humor is your best tool for dealing with them.

Sometimes interruptions come from the audience, in the form of questions and comments. I do try to minimize these by defining, in my opening remarks, how I intend to handle questions—whether I prefer people hold their questions until a certain point in the presentation or they can ask at any time. I might encourage the audience to interrupt if they don't understand an example I use, or if the information I'm presenting assumes knowledge that the audience does not have. If I've done a good job with my preparation, particularly in terms of

understanding my purpose and my audience, these circumstances seldom arise.

Occasionally, there's one person in the audience who constantly interrupts. I recently was a guest speaker at a class. The
regular instructor gave me the heads-up that there was one
person in the class who constantly asked questions. And sure
enough, I was about five minutes into the presentation when
she asked a question. It was about my topic, and I was trying to
keep it interactive, so I answered it. This led to another question, which I answered. Five minutes later, another question
came up. A few of the other students rolled their eyes.

What I quickly realized was that this person needed a lot of
attention. And there was something really passive-aggressive
about her questions. She was asking questions that were testing
my knowledge, not that moved the presentation forward. Well,
three strikes and you're out. On her third question, I responded
by saying, "You ask some really interesting questions but I have
a lot of information that I have been asked to share and I need
to respect your time. If you need me to clarify something, let
me know. Otherwise, I will be happy to talk to you after class."

At that point, I stopped looking in her direction. A few minutes later she interrupted me and asked yet another question
that was not about the presentation but was another attempt
to challenge me. "I am not going to address that question right
now," I said. "Catch me afterwards."

Of course, she did not. Without an audience for her efforts
to one-up me, she had no interest in questioning me.

Sometimes it's the audience's most important person
(MIP), the "alpha dog," who interrupts with questions that
may or may not be relevant to the topic and the presentation.
If this persists, there's only so much you can do. I politely
answer these questions, or let the MIPs make their own
proclamations. But early on when I see this pattern evolving,
I gently remind the audience that I will be addressing that

point later but want to present some background information first. Or I might gently remind the audience that we are tight on time—is it okay with them to go longer than scheduled to cover all that's on the agenda? Sometimes, you just have to roll with the audience.

When interruptions get out of hand, you may need to make a quick decision about how to handle the timing of the rest of the presentation when the interruption costs more time than is available. When this occurs, I might ask my contact or the coordinating person (or the audience, depending on the circumstances) if I can take a few extra minutes. More often, however, I must make a quick judgment call about how to best condense the remainder of the presentation.

I might do some summarizing on a section that I feel is a secondary priority. But I don't rush through any material because the audience may miss what I'm saying, and I don't skimp on the summary because that presents the key points I want my audience to take away.

INATTENTIVE AUDIENCE

There are a lot of reasons why audiences can become inattentive, and the presenter is not always the cause. When the presentation is required, then you may have some people in the audience who don't feel the material is relevant—and maybe it isn't—or who don't want to be there. Sometimes, corporate culture issues are going on. You may have been brought in by one faction but another faction was not behind them. Or there may be other issues—people are frustrated with a project, with the company, with procedures, or whatever, and can't or won't focus. Sometimes, the audience has arrived expecting one thing and you are presenting another. You may not have been adequately informed about their needs or their backgrounds.

Sometimes, the problem is the presenter. If you are not totally prepared and comfortable with yourself, are in some way distracted, or haven't created a presentation that is catching the attention of the audience, you may leave them behind. Did you set expectations at the beginning? Include an ice breaker or two to warm the audience up? Are you being yourself? Are you including examples and anecdotes that will make the presentation more interesting? Is there adequate audiovisual support, like a colorful PowerPoint presentation? Sound or video clips? These features might have helped you to maintain audience interest. If you are presenting to a group that is used to a lot of glitz in their presentations, you may be missing them solely because of that.

Again, a sense of humor helps both you and your audience. Sometimes you just have to soldier on and get through it. If you are talking about new corporate regulations, for example, you are simply talking about a topic that is not interesting except to the people who enforce them. You can't get on the side of the audience by making fun of these regulations, but if you show some interest of your own, or provide examples of why the regulations are important, or might benefit them, then you may win the audience over.

After all, a lot of boredom comes from not seeing "what's in it for me." Sometimes, you have to show the audience what's in it for them to capture their interest. What is the BENEFIT of this presentation? You may need to step back for a moment—time for one of those pauses—and figure out how to articulate that benefit. And then do it.

In a smaller group, where I can do some interacting, I like to "join the resistance." I was talking to a group of young men about a Web site for a company that produces consumer products such as bath products. I was telling them how the site would be designed and what kinds of features it would offer, and asking them for their reactions. They were yawning visibly, trying to be polite to me but also trying to stay awake.

Finally, I stopped the presentation and said, "You don't really care about this. What's missing?"

They smiled in embarrassment and surprise.

I said, "I'm not grabbing you here. Why not?"

I made it my responsibility to have let them down. This, in turn, helped me to avoid making them feel defensive. So they rallied to try and help me out. *I didn't see this. And I already know that. And why would I need to come to a Web site to see this?* The presentation became really interactive at this point, moving from a presentation to a discussion.

But I also ended up getting through the presentation. At one point, I resumed where I had stopped and we talked about what the company wanted to do, what they needed and wanted, and how compromises could be made.

In a large group, "meeting the resistance" takes a different slant. One of the ways I can use this approach is to repeatedly thank the audience for their attention. I say things like, "I know this is a lot of information at once," or, "I know this is a complete change from what you are used to," or "You may not see an advantage here . . . " or, "If you will bear with me on this, I think you will find some interesting opportunities."

By admitting that I am sensitive to how they are feeling, they at least become less resistant toward me. And then maybe they will tune in just a little bit more. We're always grateful for small progress.

ARGUMENTATIVE PARTICIPANTS

I don't argue with my audience. Some presenters do, but I believe that once you fall into an argument, you lose control of your presentation. However, I certainly do run into argumentative participants from time to time.

I did a presentation on respect in the workplace to a group of employees who were having some interpersonal issues with each other. So naturally, there were a lot of agendas in the room, and some raw feelings. One of the employees disagreed with a point that I had made. When I attempted to clarify it, he interrupted me and disagreed with my point before I had even completed it. I quickly realized that this was a no win situation because he was not mad at me, and maybe not even in disagreement with me, but he wanted to make a point in front of the other employees as well as his boss. I have to say I had to admire his guts, if not his self-destructiveness.

But I was not feeling so benevolent when he interrupted my response. I had this feeling that this could become a guy thing if I wasn't careful, and I could start to argue back. My ego was starting to become involved instinctively.

I let him finish his sentence so that I could avoid making him feel confronted. Then I smiled and said, "It looks like we're starting to go back and forth. I don't want you to think I'm argumentative. You bring up an interesting point but I can't really focus on that right now because I feel like this is going to be a larger discussion than the time we have. But I will be happy to touch base with you afterward."

He argued back. "But you don't understand. . . . "

I let him finish his sentence. I smiled again, and said, "That is a point well taken."

Then I looked away and asked another audience member, who had been smiling and nodding during the presentation, a completely unrelated question. This allowed me to introduce some positive energy back into the group. And the arguer's blustering was ignored, and so he got quiet.

I don't argue. I may try to clarify a point but if the other person does not allow me to, I acknowledge them as having an interesting point but I move on. Or I say, "I can see why you might say that." It doesn't mean they are right, but I see why they might say it anyway. Often, when the arguer realizes you are not going to take the bait, or that they are bringing up an issue that no one else has an interest in, they will be quiet.

Sometimes people just want to be acknowledged and turn into children whining for attention. They want to feel like they are also experts. If you give them the attention and validation for a moment, they will quiet down. Sometimes I encourage one of the other audience members to comment. I don't encourage two people to get into an argument. But I might seek out an expert opinion from the audience. If the arguer won't listen, or the discussion continues, I smile and suggest that they talk about it afterward—or, better yet, make dinner reservations. There's that sense of humor again!

DEFUSING HOSTILITY AND ANGER

I deal with hostile and angry people the same way as I do those who argue. A hostile person may simply sit and act sullen, or grumble, or otherwise make it a point of showing that they refuse to participate, hate being there, hate me, hate every-thing. Sometimes a hostile or angry person will be fine until called upon, and then unleash a stream of negativity that has the effect of sucking the air out of the room.

I once had a guy in a small group presentation who, when I called upon him for an opinion, let loose with a monologue of negativity about a relatively innocuous subject. My psychologist side told me that this guy was angry about stuff that had nothing to do with the topic. I finally interrupted him and said, "You bring up a lot of issues that I want to follow up on." That told him that I was done listening, but without making him feel scolded.

Then I smiled and said, "John, you don't get to go first anymore."

The other members of the audience chuckled and then he realized why I had said that, and he ended up laughing at himself. It doesn't always work this way, but I make it a point of not letting someone's anger dampen my presentation if I can avoid it. I may just ignore that person, not look in his or her direction, make sure I direct any comments toward other audience members, and not respond when he or she raises a hand. An audience member's anger is not my problem and I am not going to support it.

I have also had situations where I simply say, "You seem really angry about something here." The person can either own up to what underlies the anger and, if it is something I can answer—such as by reminding them of the focus of the presentation, or that they may not like or agree with everything they hear—that can diffuse it. Don't forget that sometimes angry people have a valid point to make and if we hear them out, we might learn something. Or we might have a chance to correct a misperception that will get the presentation back on track.

But I can't waste valuable time trying to talk people out of their anger or letting them ventilate—and neither can you. I may interrupt that person and simply say, "I am really sorry you feel that way but I have to get on with my presentation."

The person can sit and listen or leave—either is fine with me. What I don't do is fall into the trap of arguing back or being perceived as belittling the person in any way. That just throws fuel on an already raging fire, and risks making that person the underdog and me the bad guy.

Keep in mind that sometimes the presenter is a part of the team and sometimes the presenter is essentially an outsider. Even when a team member behaves badly, the other team members don't take kindly to seeing an outsider dressing him or her down.

It is amazing how far a smile, an acknowledgment that you have listened, and a firm change in direction, can take you.

In a large audience, hostile people can blend into the group and be ignored as long as you don't look in their direction. But even then, if that person seizes the floor, it is up to the presenter to seize it back, gently but firmly. "I appreciate your comments but I have to move on" will usually do the trick.

SABOTEURS

Some people just seem to want to throw you off track. They may be angry, argumentative, or just passive-aggressive. Someone may have an ax to grind about issues not related to you or the presentation. And some people may inadvertently keep interrupting or asking questions simply because they don't know any better.

As a presenter, you are expected to be an expert in the subject matter and an expert in doing presentations. The audience expects you to be in control and to stay in control. In addition to the issues like being argumentative and angry, or someone who asks a lot of questions, you may run into some audience members who want to see the presentation thrown off track for other reasons.

I was asked to do a presentation on the qualifications of my company to a client. When I got there, I noticed some tension in the room of about a dozen people. Halfway through my presentation, I started to get questions about my company's methods that seemed to be aimed at discrediting us. I felt myself being led into one trap after another—"but you just said . . . and now you are saying . . . ?"

It became clear that there were two factions in the room. Finally, I said: "I am not comfortable with the questions you are asking me. I am happy to tell you about my company's capabilities, but I feel like we are really starting to argue methodology in hypothetical situations and that doesn't seem useful to me right now. I am not sure how to respond effectively to these questions."

I saw a few looks of relief among some of the other participants. Not surprisingly, the two people firing this line of questioning at me backed off. I followed up by offering to have a discussion off-line, but that I would need to understand their objectives so that I could be better prepared. Of course, they weren't about to reveal their hidden objectives.

In other situations, I've been known to smile and say something like, "You're just determined to throw me off track today, aren't you?" This comes out like a gentle joke, but it gets the message across. Saboteurs are bullies and when they are called on their intentions, they back down.

Firmness may be necessary with others. I may look at my watch and say, "I really need to make sure I cover this material in the limited time I have. Catch me afterward."

Someone may be a saboteur by getting up and moving around, getting more coffee and doing it in a noisy manner, whispering in a loud voice to the next person. At some point, I may simply stop my presentation and watch the person. And soon, the other audience members also watch the person. Like a kid who is caught in the act, the person will soon get the message and behave.

SHOW STEALERS

Professionals are naturally competitive with each other. There's nearly always someone in the audience who feels challenged because he sees you basking in all of that attention and he wants some of it for himself. And there is the natural class clown who's been misbehaving in front of perceived authority figures his or her whole life. I find that it is best to briefly indulge these people and then ignore them.

I let them perform once and have a laugh along with everyone else. I acknowledge them for being funny or brilliant or whatever. Then I ignore them. Often, once they see that you are not going to keep indulging their need for attention, they will start to behave themselves. Ignoring may mean talking over them so that it becomes clear that you are going to drown them out and you have the podium while they don't. Or you may need to stop and say something like, "I really need to move forward here."

Once in awhile I run into someone who insists on making silly comments or corny jokes. I laugh at the first one, smile at the second one, though briefly, and then ignore them from that point onward. This usually puts an end to the behavior. I try to avoid contentiousness with one of the other audience members if at all possible. But, again, I don't let anyone take the presentation and the audience's attention away from me. After all, I am the expert and this is *my* show.

Chapter 10

Evaluating Your Success

Whew! The presentation's over, time to relax. Well, not quite—actually, now it's time to evaluate. How effective was your presentation? Did it accomplish its objectives? Did audience members leave with what they expected and needed? Feedback, assessment, and follow up are important for you, your audience, and your stakeholders (those who sponsor your presentation; I discuss this in chapter 2). Evaluation allows you to measure the success of your efforts—and it's your most powerful tool for improving your skills as a presenter.

Evaluation is the final leg of your presentation triangle, the roof of your structure. It caps everything. You might use formal assessment questionnaires and measurement tools or choose an informal evaluation process of talking with participants and stakeholders. Your client—the person who requested the presentation, whether this is your boss or an outside organization—will want to know that the time and effort of your presentation was worthwhile. After all, having you do the presentation represents an investment in you as well as for the people who attend.

THE VALUE OF FEEDBACK

Feedback gets a bad rap most of the time. Feedback represents what others think about, and how they react to, your presentation. Feedback is how you learn what you've done well, and where you could make changes or improvements that would make your presentations more effective or engaging for your audiences. Feedback, by nature, is critical—others are judging your work and assessing its value for them. It does not, however, need to be negative. Positive comments are just as important because they let you know what you're doing that's right and effective. And the truth is, you're likely doing much more of that!

Ask questions, either on a formal evaluation questionnaire or through informal dialogue with members of the audience, about what people found interesting and useful about your presentation. Solicit positive feedback; it tells you what you're doing right. Most people have plenty of positive comments to offer, and these reinforce and affirm your preparation and instincts. And I don't know about you, but I always like to hear good things about myself!

On the flip side, nobody likes to be criticized, including me, even though I've learned to look for the useful nuggets in whatever people have to say. Even when we say we want to hear what others honestly think, what we really mean is that we want to hear the good things and put our fingers in our ears for the not-so-good things. We invite critique but then brace ourselves as though for attack. It's hard not to take negative feedback personally, especially when we'd love to take positive feedback that way. We equate criticism with being picked apart (often unfairly), misunderstood, picked on, and even abused. But criticism is what makes us better presenters. We all make mistakes. I like to think that I never make the same mistake twice.

But I have to know what mistakes I've made. Unfortunately, I'm not always aware of my own mistakes, or I may do or say things that seem fine to me but are annoying to audiences, and so "talking to myself" is not a reliable way to see the problems.

Many of the presentations that I do are onsite at client companies and there is a built-in evaluation process—at the end of my presentation, I distribute an evaluation form that participants fill out anonymously. I also have evaluation forms of my own that I use when there is not one provided for me and I want to obtain written comments from the audience. Not all presentations require a formal evaluation process—more on that later in this chapter.

Creating Your Own Evaluation Forms

It's relatively easy to create your own evaluation forms. The Internet is an abundant resource for looking at the evaluation forms others use. You'll see that there's a general pattern to the questions. Look at a range of examples to stimulate your thinking about crafting your own questions. Some Web sites permit free use of their forms; when in doubt, ask for permission.

I allow the last five minutes of my presentation for audience members to complete the evaluation form, if I am using one. I ask people to leave their completed forms in a stack that is not in close proximity to me so that they don't have to worry that I will identify them when they hand it in. This safeguards privacy, which makes people feel more comfortable about being honest in their ratings and comments. Also, they fill out the evaluation on my time, not theirs. People are generally not so willing to do this on their time, despite their best intentions;

when the questionnaire walks out the door, you're not likely to see it again.

People tend to give the speaker the benefit of a doubt. If they like you and think you are a nice person, you are probably going to get higher ratings, even if the content could have been better. I try to encourage participants—either formally or informally—to include what they would've liked to have seen in the presentation, as a suggestion for future presentations. This way, they can criticize in a positive way and don't have to feel that they are putting me down. This kind of feedback also helps me to refine and update presentations that I give frequently.

But then there is, at times, someone who wants to do a hatchet job on the presenter, for any number of reasons, and you may read or hear something very negative from this person. It just happens, and more often than not it has little to do with you. A few times I've done presentations to people who really didn't want to be there, were mad at their organization, or were told that the presentation would be something else. I couldn't please them no matter what I did and the evaluations showed it. It's important to take these factors into consideration when looking at the evaluation ratings and comments. (See the section, "When Things Truly Did Go Bad," later in this chapter.)

Improve Your Public Speaking Skills

Does your community have a chapter of Toastmasters? This international organization is for people who want to improve their public speaking skills. Members present speeches of varying lengths and on different subjects, in front of the membership. It's a great way to become more confident and comfortable speaking in front of groups and also to network with other business people.

INFORMAL ASSESSMENT

Informal feedback works especially well with small groups. You can take the last few minutes of the presentation time and ask people to let you know how they think the presentation went. If you've established a rapport with them through ongoing interaction, then you may get some interesting responses.

People don't like to openly rip someone apart, especially if you are a guest or are perceived as someone in authority. But if you ask for suggestions on what else you could have discussed, or things they would like to have done in the group, you may get some helpful comments. If they clam up, then you should probably wonder whether you met their needs. Sometimes asking direct questions can elicit useful feedback. You can also invite people to contact you by phone or e-mail at a later time, giving them the option to present comments to you in a one-on-one context.

Another option is to selectively engage a few people in discussion afterward. I may approach someone who was especially interactive during the presentation. Such people are engaged and interested, and it's helpful to me to understand why and how the presentation connected with them. Sometimes it's a personal framework, for example the topic is highly relevant to the person's career or lifestyle. Other times people perceive that I understand their circumstances and can provide them with solutions to challenges they face.

Or I may approach a person who sat quietly without much participation. He or she might feel more open talking to me privately. Silence doesn't always mean the person is not getting much from the presentation; some people are simply shy about speaking out in groups. Or it could be that the topic was not what they expected. Again, I don't invite them to evaluate my performance—people don't feel qualified to do that. And sometimes it's not my performance, as such, that interests me. As I said earlier, people may really like my style but not get what they needed from the presentation. Conversely, a person may not care so much for my personality though still find a lot of value in the presentation. So I want to hear from people what they needed to hear more or less of, or what could have made it more engaging.

I always ask my contact person or stakeholder to give me feedback. Not only is this a requisite courtesy, but this person is responsible for you doing the presentation. Did your presentation meet the contact person's needs and expectations? This person may also hear comments in the days after the presentation from those who attended, or from managers who sent their people to the presentation. It's often useful to know these perceptions.

A Picture Is Worth. . . .

Videotaping yourself during a presentation can give you the opportunity to view yourself as others see you. You can directly observe your demeanor and appearance. You can see your gestures and facial expressions. And you can hear your voice. Before you set up the camera, however, get permission from your contact person or stakeholder. Tell the audience during your opening comments that you are taping your presentation for your personal improvement.

Informal feedback doesn't work so well in a larger group. The group is too large for people to feel comfortable. But I might try to connect with a few people on the way out and again, ask what they might have wanted or needed. Often, people speak to me afterward anyway. They may want to touch base and introduce themselves, or ask further questions. These encounters are further opportunities for me to get feedback. People who come to speak with you may also ask for your business card, spreading the good word about you as a presenter.

If you are presenting to members of your own organization, you may not get great informal feedback. Office politics may prevent your colleagues from feeling comfortable in giving honest feedback, but politics may also prevent them from being as complimentary as they might be. Feedback may come back to you as a delayed reaction—through someone else, or in a casual conversation. But if your boss is involved in any way, I suggest you make an attempt to pull him or her aside and ask for feedback. Bosses usually have something to say.

STRUCTURED ASSESSMENT

It's common to use an evaluation form at the end of the presentation, whether it is a large or small group. These may not be used beyond a chance for you to glance over them and see if any problems are highlighted. Or they may be part of a more formal process of evaluating you. If you are doing a presentation within your own company the results may end up in your file, or be used to determine whether you are asked back if you are presenting to an outside group.

Generally, various aspects of the presentation are rated on a five- or ten-point scale, with space for comments. Each item on such an evaluation form usually should be a single sentence that conveys a single point. Response to the statement, "The presenter was professional and spoke loudly enough to be heard in the back of the room," could give you useful information but will you know about what? Better to break such a statement into two items. Incorporating two points in one item only works when the two relate to each other. Terms such as "professional" are also subjective—what is professional to me may not seem so to an audience that has characteristics in common that I don't share.

Comments can be tricky. You tend to get comments from people who either loved or hated your presentation, and not so many in between. Keep in mind that you may be hearing from the extremes but not from the majority, so don't be thrown off in either direction by these comments and remind any others involved in looking at the evaluations that they should take the same perspective. And people aren't natural writers, often, so they aren't even comfortable taking the time to write comments. Most of the time people are in such a hurry to get out of the room that they don't take much time on the evaluation anyway.

The evaluation is always a wild card for me. I like to have a lot of control, and I don't have much of any control here. I do make sure the evaluation includes questions that separate what the audience liked or didn't like about various aspects of the presentation—content, format, visual aids, environment, presenter. This way, the whole presentation doesn't get slammed just because someone thought the room was too hot or didn't like the use of video clips. On the other hand, I invite the audience members to evaluate me as a presenter, separate from the presentation. That is a risk I have to take so that the evaluation is fair and comprehensive. Someone may dislike my personal style for some reason, but if the person still got value from the presentation, then that is a good thing.

Generally, the stakeholders—the people, such as clients or bosses, who arrange the presentations—are responsible for collecting and tabulating the evaluation forms. Or I may collect the completed evaluations but turn them over or send them to the stakeholder. But I do ask for a chance to read through them or to at least get the tabulation. If I'm doing two of the same presentations in a row, I may not want to see the evaluation forms from the first presentation before I do the second presentation. I need to stay focused on what I need to present to the next group, and I don't want to be distracted from that.

SAMPLE EVALUATION FORMS

Here are two sample evaluation forms that I use in my presentations. Feel free to photocopy them to use in your presentations, or to adapt them to meet your specific needs. Notice I do include space for comments even when I use a numeric scale evaluation. I do this because people who have more to say will write it on the form anyway, so incorporating a comment opportunity into each question lets me shape the relevance of the comments. You can use a numeric scale without comments if you prefer.

Sample Evaluation Form #1: Numeric Scale with Comments

Your feedback is important to us. Please take a few moments to share your assessment of this training program with us by indicating your responses to the questions listed below. Please respond by circling the appropriate number on a scale of one to five, with one being poor and five being good. Feel free to add any comments.

1. **The purpose of this program was clearly stated and the objectives were met.**

    (poor)   1   2   3   4   5   (good)

    Comment:
    ....
    ....

2. **The material was presented in an understandable format.**

    (poor)   1   2   3   4   5   (good)

    Comment:
    ....
    ....
    ....

3. **The supporting materials and handouts were relevant.**

       (poor)   1   2   3   4   5 (good)

Comment: ....

4. **The use of audiovisual support was effective.**

       (poor)   1   2   3   4   5 (good)

Comment: ....
....

5. **I can apply what I learned today to my specific job or life situation.**

       (poor)   1   2   3   4   5 (good)

Comment: ....
....
....

6. **The instructor was effective at leading the class and holding my interest.**

       (poor)   1   2   3   4   5 (good)

Comment: ....
....
....

7. **The room was comfortable and facilitated the learning experience.**

       (poor)   1   2   3   4   5 (good)

Comment: ....
....

Sample Evaluation Form #2: Narrative Responses
Write in your responses and comments for each question.

1. **Specifically, what concepts, issues, or discussions did you find helpful during the presentation?**

   ....

   ....

2. **List three ways you can apply the information that was presented:**

   ....

   ....

3. **What changes to the workshop would you recommend? Anything you would like to see more of? Less of?**

   ....

   ....

4. **Any other topics you would like to see presented in the future?**

   ....

   ....

5. **Additional comments and suggestions:**

   ....

   ....

FOLLOW UP WITH PARTICIPANTS

Whether, and how, you follow up with participants depends on many variables. If I know any of the participants, I will definitely give them a call within a few days of the presentation to see if they have any feedback. This will just be a casual call. If I know them well, I will ask them to be honest and comment on my style as well as the content and organization of the recent presentation. I may have specific concerns I want to ask about. If I don't know them well, I will just ask them to let me know if there is anything that could have been different, and see where that leads.

Really Follow Up

When you tell someone you'll get back to him or her, make sure to do so—and in a timely manner. If you don't know the person, get contact information at the end of your presentation. If it will take you time to get back, let the person know. If you can't find the answer, let the person know that, too.

Sometimes I get a question that I can't answer. I may tell the person that I'll get an answer and get back to that specific person or to the stakeholder. Either way, I make a note of that question and I do get the answer and follow up. Both participants and stakeholders really appreciate this effort. If someone comes up to me after the presentation and asks a question, or makes reference to something I said, if I promise to follow up with them, I make sure I do that. You still have opportunities to leave a lasting impression after the presentation is over. Following up is one of them.

FOLLOW UP WITH STAKEHOLDERS

The opinions of your stakeholders—those who requested you do the presentation—are important for you to know whether you met the presentation's desired objectives. You can follow up with stakeholders formally and informally. If you're working with peers or coworkers, then the follow up helps you build and solidify relationships. It also enhances your image as a leader. This may mean making sure the presentation met their needs or addressing any further questions. I may send this kind of follow up in the form of an e-mail, bring it up at a meeting, or mention it in casual encounters.

Sometimes it's more appropriate to defer to your boss on this. The department head may want to talk to other departments about the presentation, rather than having the presenter initiate those contacts. It is important to ask your boss what kind of follow he or she wants you to do. There are always perceptions and office politics at stake here.

If I'm working with a company or an organization, I send a formal thank-you note or letter, or an e-mail if that is the way we have been communicating, to let them know that I appreciated the opportunity to present and enjoyed working with them. I might highlight something that happened during or after the presentation, such as whether the audience asked a lot of questions, to remind them that it was a success.

With client company or organization, this is an opportunity for you to brand yourself. Use a well written letter, printed on your letterhead, and even include a brochure or business card. This will again remind the organization of what you have to offer. Someone will file away your information, and when other needs arise you'll be right there, so to speak, to step up for the assignment.

You might also want to send a hardcopy of the handouts you used during your presentation, or a printed transcript of your presentation, just to make your stakeholders have access to them. If you've been communicating by e-mail, you can attach files to your thank-you e-mail. Did you carefully brand yourself—name, address, company, e-mail, phone—on the front page of the presentation and any other printed materials? It's common for clients to forget your name but remember your presentation.

I always offer to answer any further questions, and solicit additional comments, from the stakeholders. I generally ask:

- How did I help you?
- Is there anything else I could have done?
- Is there anything else you need now?

Such an approach reminds the stakeholders that I am on their team, even if I don't work with them every day. This sense of connection is important, particularly if I'm likely, or I want, to do more presentations for these stakeholders.

Stakeholders do not always have helpful feedback, either. Sometimes they realize after the presentation that they did not give you the best guidance to prepare the presentation. I have had a stakeholder admit that I had been given one direction when I should have been given another. Or I may find that the recommendations I made had been vetted by my stakeholder but not the stakeholder's boss, and the boss didn't like them. The stakeholder may or may not support you, often depending on circumstances you know nothing about. And if you are the outsider, you may be made a scapegoat. Fortunately, this is relatively rare.

WHEN THINGS TRULY DID GO BADLY

It happens to all of us at some point . . . things go bad. Sometimes the causes are beyond your control, and sometimes they happen despite your control. Usually you know that circumstances are slipping away from you, which often makes it worse. You know, but you seem unable to do anything to stop the slide. Generally, a cascade of events develops when a presentation totally tanks. Professionals in many fields, from lawyers to teachers to public safety personnel, conduct debriefings after key events to assess what worked, what went wrong, why, and how to manage future events more appropriately and effectively.

Events beyond your control may include computer failure, equipment malfunctions, environmental factors (room too hot or too cold, lighting problems, seating arrangements), and even audience configuration. Keeping your cool and your sense of humor go a long way toward making the most of the situation while it's unfolding (chapter 9 discusses ways to deal with challenges during your presentation) but afterward, the evaluations can help you ferret out the problems. Approach this constructively—you will learn from this experience, and hopefully you won't ever repeat it.

Events within your control that slip away from you may include mistakes on materials and handouts, missing pages, forgotten supplies, time and timing issues, and audience interaction. With most of these events, you'll be able to identify the turning point. Were the handouts late getting back from the print shop and you didn't have time to proof them? Was someone else supposed to prepare and review materials? Did you get delayed at the airport or stuck in traffic? Lessons from the answers to such questions can help you prevent repeats of mistakes.

Looking back with the perfect vision of hindsight, ask yourself:

- What, exactly, went wrong?
- When did it start to go wrong?
- What allowed the initiating event to cascade into disaster?
- Is there anything I could've done to prevent or mitigate mistakes?
- Is there any way I could've prepared for the twist that sank me?

You won't always be able to answer these questions. Your audience may get out of control, for example, for reasons that never become clear and that may or may not have anything to do with you or the presentation. Sometimes there truly was nothing you could've done to avert disaster. Most importantly, look for the lessons and then put it behind you. You bombed. It's okay. Your next presentation is a fresh start. Go back to the basics (chapters 1 through 9), then go out and do the best you can.

INCORPORATING IMPROVEMENTS

Not all of the comments I get in feedback about my presentations are useful. Sometimes they don't make any sense at all. For example, someone may suggest that I go much more in depth on a topic that was too far flung. Or a person suggests video clips or music when that much audiovisual support would not have been feasible.

Even so, I try to go through any suggestions I receive with my mind as open as possible. This isn't always easy. When you work really hard on a presentation, you have a depth of involvement that makes it hard not to be defensive. How can you allow your "child" to be subjected to such unfair criticism? I try to remind myself that a presentation is a product. I created it, sure, but it is not me. It is separate from me. And so when what I feel like are darts being thrown at that product, I can maintain a distance that allows me to better evaluate which darts should stick and which should be immediately removed and discarded.

I did a presentation on work-life balance. I worked hard on the presentation; this is a key topic in today's workplace. So I talked a lot about why this is in many ways an unrealistic presentation and how important it is to maintain a positive attitude and not beat ourselves up for sometimes working too hard. I talked about how to relax and de-stress. And then I briefly covered a few points about how to add more balance.

Later the stakeholder approached me. As we were walking out, she said, "They really liked you and thought you were interesting. But they had hoped to learn more tips on how to create more balance in their own lives." And she gave me some examples from her experiences.

I was kind of annoyed at first. By my way of thinking, attitude is more important than techniques or methods that may or may not be relevant to everyone. And just how many people had she talked to, anyway? I listened politely and then thanked her for her comments.

A day or so later, after I had some distance, I thought about what she had said and I decided she did make some valid points. I probably had done too much psychologizing when the people in the audience just needed a few ideas to help them get some balance in their life. That's really all they wanted. Now when I do this kind of presentation, I include specific suggestions and methods. I ask questions of the audience to learn what issues trouble them the most, and I tailor my information to target those issues. Even when I think I understand my audience, I ask these questions as part of my presentation. I know what I think the audience needs to know, but I'm not always right. If I'm not meeting their needs, then I am not doing my job. Perception *is* reality.

However, don't underestimate the value of distance. Sometimes as presenters we take such ownership and this is a double-edged sword. By feeling like we have some skin in the game, we work that much harder. But we may not be open to feedback because we are so invested. The presentation has become an extension of who we are, and then we may not have distance. Give yourself a few days to let feedback sink in, if you can. And then evaluate it as if your presentation was a product and you want to make sure the next version is even better. In this way, it's nothing personal.

ON TO THE NEXT PRESENTATION!

The more you do presentations, the better at it you become. Remember, this is a learning continuum—and you learn as you go. You'll have wonderful successes and you'll have some duds, this is the way it goes. As hard as it may be at times, look for the lessons buried in the duds. Harsh criticisms hurt, but sometimes they result in remarkable breakthroughs to the next level. And positive support goes even further, inspiring confidence and even enjoyment as you do more presentations.

If you're going to be doing more presentations—and why wouldn't you, now that you're getting good at it?—then it's worth your time and effort to improve your public speaking and presentation skills. The Internet is a vast resource for information and tips as well as articles, books, and specific topics. Many communities have chapters of Toastmasters International, a membership organization dedicated public speaking. Your community may have other organizations that focus on or emphasize public speaking and related subjects. And consider a return to the classroom—colleges and universities have courses on communication, public speaking, presentation design, psychology, and other topics that can help you hone your skills.

Read. There are dozens, if not hundreds, of books on all different aspects of presentations and public speaking—some very narrowly focused on specific audiences, some look at the psychology of group interactions, some explore the fear of speaking in front of groups. Appendix B provides further reading recommendations to get you started.

Go to other presentations to see how other people do them. You'll learn from both the good things and the not-so-good things that people do. Go to presentations of all kinds, even on topics that don't particularly interest you. You can concentrate more on the presenter when you're not so interested in the subject matter. You may discover, in watching someone else, that you have the same habits you find yourself doing (like clicking a pen!). You can see, too, how the presenter's gestures and appearance can either support or detract from the presentation. Libraries, local governments and agencies, civic organizations, and community groups are great resources for free presentations. And you may even volunteer to do presentations in these settings on subjects that interest you, for the fun of it!

Appendix A

Resources

These organizations provide valuable resources and information for public speakers:

Academy for Professional Speaking
www.academyforprofessionalspeaking.org

American Speakers Bureau
www.speakersbureau.com

International Federation for Professional Speaker
www.iffps.org

National Speakers Association
www.nsaspeaker.org

Toastmasters International
www.toastmasters.org

Appendix B

Further Reading

Atkinson, Cliff. *Beyond Bullet Points: Using Microsoft PowerPoint to Create Presentations That Inform, Motivate, and Inspire.* Redmond, WA: Microsoft Press, 2005.

Business Communication (Harvard Business Essentials). Boston, MA: Harvard Business School Press, 2003.

Dempsey, David J., JD. *Better to Best: How to Speak for Extraordinary Results . . . Every Time!* Atlanta, GA: Miranda Publishing, LLC, 2006.

Few, Stephen. *Show Me the Numbers: Designing Tables and Graphs to Enlighten.* Oakland, CA: Analytics Press, 2004.

Laskowski, Lenny. *10 Days to More Confident Public Speaking.* New York, NY: Warner Books, 2001.

Lucas, Stephen E. *The Art of Public Speaking.* New York, NY: McGraw-Hill, 2007.

Mayer, Richard E. *Multimedia Learning.* Cambridge, UK: Cambridge University Press, 2001.

Strunk, William Jr., and E. B. White. *The Elements of Style, Fourth Edition.* Needham Heights, MA: Allyn & Bacon, 2000.

van Oech, Roger. *A Whack on the Side of the Head: How You Can Be More Creative, Third Edition.* New York, NY: Warner Business Books, 1998.

Wempen, Faithe. *PowerPoint Advanced Presentation Techniques.* Indianapolis, IN: John Wiley & Sons, 2004.

Quotations for Speeches

Presenters find it's helpful to borrow the words of others to begin or close their remarks, to make a point, or to add a little humor or poignancy. Good presenters keep a stash of pithy or pointed quotations to put some spice into their mix of words. This appendix provides you with a diverse collection of quotations, sayings, and nuggets.

When using a quotation, you may want to introduce it with one of the following phrases:

- A wise person once said . . .
- (Name of person quoted) once said . . .
- I read that . . .
- I've heard that . . .
- Someone once said . . .

Some quotations contain somewhat archaic or stilted language. And older quotations often contain the words he, him, man, and so forth, making them potentially offensive to those who are sensitive to gender bias in language. The Task Force on Bias-Free Language suggests that direct quotes should not be altered in scholarly writing. But the members of the task force also understand that this is a problem for those writers who use quotations that contain biased language.

Since this book is not specifically geared to the scholarly presenter, I suggest that careful editing be applied to these witty, sage, or insightful quotations so that they will fit your needs. I have taken the liberty of changing some of the quotations listed in this appendix in an effort to pass along words that will not offend. (The edited quotations are marked with an asterisk.)

If you feel the need to acknowledge any changes you make in someone's quotation, you might say:

- (Name) once offered this advice.
- I read something that impressed me. It goes something like this.
- There's an old saying that goes something like this.
- To paraphrase (name) . . .

It is my hope that a few of the following quotations will be appropriate for your presentation and will enhance what you have to say:

The world judges you by what you have done, not by what you have started out to do; by what you have completed, not by what you have begun. The bulldog wins by the simple expedient of holding on to the finish.

—BALTASAR GRACIAN

The first principle of achievement is mental attitude. People begin to achieve when they begin to believe.

—J. C. ROBERTS

1. *Do more than exist, live.*
2. *Do more than touch, feel.*
3. *Do more than look, observe.*

4.   *Do more than read, absorb.*

5.   *Do more than hear, listen.*

6.   *Do more than listen, understand.*

7.   *Do more than think, ponder.*

8.   *Do more than talk, say something.*

—John H. Rhoades

Measure twice, saw once.

—Anonymous

Talk low, talk slow and don't say too much.

—Texas Bix Binder

No one is more confusing than the person who gives good advice while setting a bad example.

—Booker T. Washington

You never know what is enough until you know what is more than enough.

—William Blake

Chance favors the prepared mind.

—Louis Pasteur

The obvious is that which is never seen until someone expresses it simply.

—Kahlil Gibran

A vocabulary of truth and simplicity will be of service through-out life.

— WINSTON CHURCHILL

We boil at different degrees.

— RALPH WALDO EMERSON

What is easy is seldom excellent.

— SAMUEL JOHNSON

A sense of humor is a sense of proportion.

— KAHLIL GIBRAN

Funny how people despise platitudes, when they are usually the truest thing going. A thing has to be pretty true before it gets to be a platitude.

— KATHARINE F. GEROULD

Time has no divisions to make its passage. There is never a thunderstorm or blare of trumpets to announce the beginning of a new month or year. Even when a new century begins, it is only we mortals who ring bells. . . .

— THOMAS MANN

Always do right; this will gratify some people and astonish the rest.

— MARK TWAIN

I praise loudly; I blame softly.

—CATHERINE II OF RUSSIA

No one ever makes us mad. We grow angry as a result of our own choice.

—ANONYMOUS

The torrid sun melts mountain snows.

When anger comes, then wisdom goes.

—CHINESE SAYING

Swallowing angry words is better than choking on an apology.

—ANONYMOUS

There are no great people; only great challenges that ordinary people are forced by circumstances to meet.

—ANONYMOUS

Happiness adds and multiples as we divide it with others.

—ANONYMOUS

Never bend your head. Always hold it high.

Look the world straight in the eye.

—HELEN KELLER

By appreciation we make excellence in others our own property.

—Voltaire

The power of persistence, of enduring defeat and of gaining victory by defeats, is one of those forces which never loses its charm.

—Ralph Waldo Emerson

The most difficult thing in the world is to appreciate what we have—until we lose it.

—Anonymous

The strongest words are often used in the weakest arguments.

—Anonymous

After eating an entire bull, a mountain lion felt so good he started roaring. He kept it up until a hunter came along and shot him. The moral: When you're full of bull, keep your mouth shut.

—Texas Bix Binder

He has achieved success who has lived well, laughed often and loved much.

—Bessie Anderson

There is no sin except stupidity.

—Oscar Wilde

In this world there are only two tragedies. One is not getting what one wants, and the other is getting it.

—OSCAR WILDE

I am seeking only to face realities and to face them without soft concealments.

—WOODROW WILSON

If we want a thing badly enough, we can make it happen. If we let ourselves be discouraged, that is proof that our wanting was inadequate.

—DOROTHY SAYERS

Read every day something no one else is reading. Think something no one else is thinking. It is bad for the mind to be always a part of unanimity.

—CHRISTOPHER MORLEY

As a rule indeed, grown-up people are fairly correct on matters of fact; it is in the higher gift of imagination that they are so sadly to seek.

—KENNETH GRAHAME

Those who bring sunshine to the lives of others cannot keep it from themselves.

—JAMES BARRIE

When there are two people in a business who always agree, one of them is unnecessary.

—WILLIAM WRIGLEY, JR.

The easiest way to eat crow is while it's still warm. The colder it gets, the harder it is to swaller.

—TEXAS BIX BINDER

You ain't heard nothin' yet, folks.

—AL JOLSON

They say that life is a highway and its milestones are the years.

—JOYCE KILMER

Diplomacy is to do and say

The nastiest thing in the nicest way.

—ISAAC GOLDBERG

Politics is the science of how who gets what, when and why.

—SIDNEY HILLMAN

I'd rather have an inch of dog than miles of pedigree.

—DANA BURNET

Nothing changes more constantly than the past; for the past that influences our lives does not consist of what actually happened, but of what we believe happened.

—GERALD WHITE JOHNSON

Each honest calling, each walk of life, has its own elite, its own aristocracy based on excellence of performance.

—JAMES BRYANT CONANT

Believe it or not.

—ROBERT RIPLEY

Baloney is flattery so thick it cannot be true, and blarney is flattery so thin we like it.

—FULTON JOHN SHEEN

I had to sink my yacht to make my guests go home.

—F. SCOTT FITZGERALD

If you find yourself in a hole, the first thing to do is stop diggin'.

—TEXAS BIX BINDER

The way of the future is coming and there is no fighting it.

—ANNE MORROW LINDBERGH

What is past is prologue.

—WILLIAM SHAKESPEARE

I hate quotations! Tell me what you know.
—RALPH WALDO EMERSON

When you have eliminated the impossible, whatever remains, however improbable, must be the truth.
—SIR ARTHUR CONAN DOYLE

The human body is an instrument for the production of art in the life of the human soil.
—ALFRED NORTH WHITEHEAD

The materials of action are variable, but the use we make of them should be constant.
—EPICTETUS (C. 60 A.D.)

Remember this, that there is a proper dignity and proportion to be observed in the performance of every action in life.
—MARCUS AURELIUS

Look beneath the surface; let not the several qualities of a thing nor its worth escape thee.
—MARCUS AURELIUS

Look to the essence of a thing, whether it be a point of doctrine, of practise, or of interpretation.
—MARCUS AURELIUS

Never invest your money in anything that eats or needs repainting.

—Billy Rose

If a man has good corn or wood or boards or pigs to sell, or can make better chairs or knives, crucibles, or church organs, than anybody else, you will find a broad, hard-beaten path to his house, though it be in the woods.

—Ralph Waldo Emerson

It is better to ask some of the questions than to know all the answers.

—James Thurber

There are six big reasons why people find their way into top management positions:

They know how to manage others.

They know how to read what is behind the figures of the business.

They think simply.

Problems never take them by surprise.

They have imagination about the public.

They have faith in human nature.

—Robert R. Updegraff

There would be plenty of sympathy if people would spread it around instead of using it all on themselves.

—ANONYMOUS

Tact fails the moment it is noticed.

—EDWARD LONGSTRETH

If the power to do hard work is not talent, it is the best possible substitute for it.

—ANONYMOUS

A teacher who is attempting to teach without inspiring the pupil with a desire to learn is hammering on cold iron.

—HORACE MANN

The giant oak is an acorn that held its ground.

—ANONYMOUS

Lose an hour in the morning and you will be looking for it the rest of the day.

—LORD CHESTERFIELD

Remember, even a kick in the caboose is a step forward.

—TEXAS BIX BINDER

No man-made weapon has been devised so lethal, potent or dangerous as words wrongly used.

—LARRY DORST

Happiness makes up in height for what it lacks in length.

—ROBERT FROST

Speed is good when wisdom clears the way.

—EDWARD R. MURROW

Hell is truth seen too late.

—ALEXANDER ADAM

I leave this rule for others when I'm dead,

Be always sure you're right—then go ahead.

—DAVY CROCKETT

If life had a second edition, how I would correct the proofs.

—JOHN CLARE

All work is as seed sown; it grows and spreads, and sows itself anew.

—THOMAS CARLYLE

Nothing great was ever achieved without enthusiasm.

—RALPH WALDO EMERSON

Dogmatism is puppyism come to its full growth.
—DOUGLAS JERROLD

Never ask a barber if he thinks you need a haircut.
—TEXAS BIX BINDER

It is much easier to be critical than to be correct.
—BENJAMIN DISRAELI

If you call a tail a leg, how many legs has a dog? Five? No; calling a tail a leg don't make it a leg.
—ABRAHAM LINCOLN

After the verb "To Love," "To Help" is the most beautiful verb in the world.
—BARONESS BERTHA VON SUTTNER

Even a thought, even a possibility can shatter us and transform us.
—FRIEDRICH WILHELM NIETZSCHE

To know is nothing at all; to imagine is everything.
—ANATOLE FRANCE

It is difference of opinion that makes horse races.
—MARK TWAIN

A classic is something that everybody wants to have read and nobody wants to read.

—MARK TWAIN

If you hit a pony over the nose at the outset of your acquaintance, he may not love you, but he will take a deep interest in your movements ever afterwards.

—RUDYARD KIPLING

Luck is good when it isn't bad.

—ANONYMOUS

Paying attention to simple little things that most people neglect makes a few people rich.

—HENRY FORD

All life is an experiment. The more experiments you make, the better.

—RALPH WALDO EMERSON

Index

A

Academy for Professional
  Speaking, 187
American Speakers Bureau, 187
Anecdotes/stories, 52–54
Appearance, appropriate, 80
Assessment, informal, 171–73
Assessment, structured, 173–75
Atkinson, Cliff, 189
Attire, 79–82
Audience, 16
  anecdotes/stories for,
  52–54
  greeting your, 134–36
  hidden, 37–39
  inattentive, 157–59
  know your, 21–22, 28
  level of, 62
  as mandatory
  attendees, 33–35
  needs of, 22, 33, 36–37,
  49
  participation, 143–45
  peers as, 23–37
  remote, 35–36
  stakeholders as, 37–39
  subordinates as,
  30–32
  superiors as, 27–30
  test, 99–100

topic knowledge of,
  43–44
virtual and, 100
willing participants
  as, 32–33
Audiovisual elements, 116–17
*A Whack on the Side of the
  Head: How You Can Be More
  Creative* (van Oech), 190

B

Background, 49, 50, 75
Benefits, 6
*Better to Best: How to Speak
  for Extraordinary Results . . .
  Every Time!* (Dempsey), 189
*Beyond Bullet Points: Using
  Microsoft PowerPoint to
  Create Presentations That
  Inform, Motivate, and Inspire*
  (Atkinson), 189
Breathing, 142
Business casual, 81
Business Communications, 189
Buzzwords, 51–52

C

Challenges, 25–27, 29–30, 31–32
Challenges, handling, 151–65
  argumentative
  participants and,
  159–61

inattentive audience and, 157–59

interruptions and, 155–57

latecomers and, 153–55

saboteurs and, 163–64

sense of humor and, 151–53, 158, 161

show-stealers and, 164–65

Checklists, pre-presentation, 109–29

arrival at venue and, 123–25

audiovisual elements and, 116–17

confirmations and, 119–21

contingency planning and, 128–29

details and, 109, 110

handouts and, 114–15

logistical details, 121–26

mailing/shipping and, 121–22

onsite support and, 125–26

presenter's tool bag and, 127–28

production schedule and, 112–19

related people/tasks and, 118–19

supplies and, 126–27

travel and, 122–23

Concluding presentation, 148–49

Copyright matters, 54–55

Credentials, 47

Credibility, establishing, 138

Criticism, 168

D

Demeanor, 83–85

Dempsey, David J., 189

Details, 109, 110

Development process, 93, 94

Dress rehearsals, 105–6

E

Educational presentations, 12–13

Egos, 25, 26

Elements, essential, 141

The Elements of Style (Strunk and White), 190

Emotions/passion, 102–3

Evaluation, 167–85

feedback and, 168–70

following up, 177–78

forms, 169, 173, 175–77

incorporating improvements and, 182–84

informal assessment and, 171–73

structured assessment
and, 173–75
Expectations, 7–8
Expectations, establishing,
136–38
Experience, personal, 5–6
Expertise, 4–5
Eye contact, 141–42

F

Feedback, 168–70, 171, 172, 173,
177
Few, Stephen, 189
Flip charts, 142
Following up, 178
Foundation triangle, 2, 21, 41
Framework, 63
Fundamentals, 2

G

Google, 46
Ground rules, establishing,
145–47

H

Handout checklist, 115, 117
Handouts, 70–72, 114–15
Humor, sense of, 151–53, 158,
161

I

Improvements, incorporating,
182–84
Insecurities, 79
Interaction, etiquette for, 36
Interactions, reinforce, 144

International Speakers
Association, 187
Internet, 22, 46
Interruptions, 155–57
Introduction, 138–40
Introduction, content, and
conclusion, 63–66

J

Jealousies, 25

K

Knowledge level, 5

L

Laskowski, Lenny, 189

M

Man on the moon test, 37, 74, 89
Mannerisms, 103–5
Mayer, Richard E., 189
Media options, 67–70
Most important person (MIP),
28, 84, 154, 156
Multimedia Learning (Mayer),
189
Multimedia presentations, 69

O

Objectives, 7–8, 64
Office politics, 173, 179
"Off-the-cuff," 90
Outlines, 70

P

Pacing, 142–43
Participants, argumentative,
159–61

Participants, follow up with, 177–78

Perspective, keeping, 4

Persuasive presentations, 17–18

Plagiarism, 54

Posture, 101

PowerPoint, ix, 36, 45, 64, 69, 70, 71, 72, 73

PowerPoint Advanced Presentation Techniques (Wempen), 190

Practice, 87–90, 93

Preparation triangle, 77, 93

Presentation checklist, 113

Presentations, anecdotes/stories for, 52–54

Presentations, art/science of, ix–x

Presentation's delivery, 140–43

Presentations, developing, 57–76
comfort zone and, 62–63
determining style and, 57–61
framework of and, 63–66
handouts and, 70–72
introduction, content, and conclusion and, 63–66
media options, 67–70
notes for, 72–74
preparing for questions/challenges and, 74–76
style strengths and weaknesses, 60–61
time/environment considerations and, 66–67
visual components and, 72

Presentations, peer reviews of, 25

Presentations, practicing, 87–90

Presentations, types of, 8–19
educational, 12–13
informational, 9–15
motivational, 15–17
multimedia, 69
persuasive, 17–18
reports and, 11–12
sales, 18–19
training, 13–15, 64, 71, 146

Presenter, preparation of, 77–91
being the expert and, 77–79
be yourself, 85–87
demeanor and, 83–85
mind your manners, 85
practicing presentations and, 87–90
what to wear? and, 79–82

Privacy, protecting, 52, 53, 69

Production details, 112

Production schedule, 112–19

Public speaking skills, 170

Purpose, 3, 7, 8, 9, 10

Q

Questions, fielding, 145–47

Quotations from speeches, 191–201

R

Read-through, first complete, 94

Rehearsals, 93–108

    appearance and, 94

    dress, 105–6

    emotions/passion and, 102–3

    first run: read-through (timing), 94–97

    gaps/glitches and, 107–8

    handling questions and, 97

    podium factor, 101

    second run: how do you sound (sound check) and, 97–103

    sound check and, 94, 97–103

    test audience and, 99–100

    third run: how do you look (looks) and, 103–6

    timing and, 93, 94–97

    virtual audience and, 100

    visual components and, 103–6

    voice projection/volume and, 100–102

    volume/tonal quality and, 98

Relevance, 10

Reports, 11–12

Research, 46–49

Research formats, styles, and approaches, 48–49

Resistance, meeting the, 34, 35, 159

S

Saboteurs, 163–64

Sales presentations, 18–19

Self-doubt, 79

Self talk, 78, 79

Semi-casual clothes, 82

Setup arrangements, 131–34

Show Me the Numbers: Designing Tables and Graphs to Enlighten (Few), 189

Show-stealers, 164–65

Skepticism, 47–48

Sources, know your, 50

Stakeholders, 37–39, 174, 178–80, 183

Strunk, William Jr., 190

Style, determining, 57–61

Style, strengths/weaknesses, 60–61

About the Author

GARY MCCLAIN, PH.D., is a counselor and research consultant in New York City, with 25 years of experience as a mental health professional and in the business world. He has published numerous books and articles and has recently launched a healthcare Web site, *www.JustGotDiagnosed.com.*